A Stake in Tomorrow

World Class Lessons

in

Business Partnerships

A Stake in Tomorrow

World Class Lessons

in

Business Partnerships

by

John Marsh

B. T. BATSFORD LIMITED · LONDON

© John Marsh 1998
First published 1998

Published by B T Batsford Ltd,
583 Fulham Road,
London SW6 5BY

Printed by
Redwood Books
Trowbridge
Wiltshire

ISBN 0 7134 8366 0

A CIP catalogue record for this book
is available from The British Library

Contents

This book is dedicated to Richard and Robert in the hope that they may grow up to have a real stake in their futures.

Figures

Table

Table	Description	Page

Acknowledgements

Many people and organisations have contributed directly or indirectly to this book. I am indebted to all of them, in particular my business partner, Martin Sandbrook and all of my clients. Thanks to Jackie, Jeanie and Sue for their support and belief in the ideals contained within this book. They kept me going through the troughs that all authors experience.

I would like to acknowledge the following people and organisations explicitly.

Avon Ambulance Service
Army Technical Support Agency
CAPITEC
Central England EBP
Choices for Bristol
D2D
East Wiltshire Health Care Trust
Essex Training and Enterprise Council
John Jay Bostingl, Schools of Quality, USA
John Tidball, TQM
John Winters, BT Batsford
Pearce Construction Group PLC
Harvey Stewart, VP Foundation for Community Vitality
Hemmings Waste Management
ICL
Marks & Spencer
Mount Edgecumbe High School, Sitka, Alaska, USA
Royal Crescent Hotel

Royal National Hospital for Rheumatic Diseases
Smith's Wood Partnership
St John the Baptist Primary School
Safer Surrey Partnership
Surrey Care Trust
Quality in the Community, Bristol, UK

The book was written in the very conducive locations of Honolulu, Hawaii; Skibbereen, Republic of Ireland; Dyffryn, Wales; and Rio, Brazil. Thanks to all those who gave me support in these communities.

Finally thanks to all those who by their hard work and vision are taking stakeholding from a political/managerial concept to a practical reality.

Foreword

JCP is an organization committed to co-operation, and facilitating about 80 partnerships a year across business and community organizations.

Occasionally, a giant will stride into your life who will pick you up by your heels and shake out your lazy, unimaginative thoughts about work, organizations and people. He will then drop you on your backside to try to pick up all the new thoughts and to make useful sense of them — while trying to cling on to his coat tails to catch the next dose of wisdom.

Such a man was the late, great, Dr Deming. What he gave to many of us was a new paradigm; a great deal of confusion and even more hope. What he left behind was a vision of organizational life based on one key principle — Interdependence — and a scattered bunch of enlightened people who were determined to try to implement his vision.

John Marsh is one of these. *A Stake in Tomorrow* is a successful attempt to demonstrate the negative effects of competitive thinking — fragmentation — and to give practical steps to the new interdependence paradigm for the whole of society. His passion is the community, which is the dumping ground of what Dr Deming called *"the disastrous effects for people who are living under the tyranny of the prevailing style of management"*.

This is a book, therefore, for everyone to read who wants to make a difference. It is, above all, a hopeful book.

John Carlisle
President, JCP
November 1997

Part 1

Theory of Stakeholding

Chapter 1

Why Stakeholding?

The State We're In

The title for this section is borrowed from Will Hutton's exceptional book published in 1995. In this book Hutton defines the systemic problems faced by the British State and the British Economy (1). Many of these problems are shared with other Western nations, particularly ones based on Anglo-Saxon history and culture. The very problems these nations face are a result of their prevalent ways of thinking and hence managing. If they continue with the same methods they will continue to get the same results. Fundamentally different approaches are required but before these are explored the old ones, and their failings, need to be understood.

Western nations are facing a crisis. Once confident peoples are now feeling insecure and a sense of desperation is becoming endemic. The symptoms are legion, including:

- Soaring balance of payments deficits.
- Long-term unemployment.
- Ever increasing crime rates.
- Widening gaps between wealthy and poor.
- The emergence of an underclass.
- Rising prison populations.
- Job insecurity.
- Lack of faith in institutions and their leaders.
- Trends towards fundamentalism.

- Greater inequalities of opportunity.
- Declining social services.
- Loss of workers' rights.
- A general sense of hopelessness and despair.

The overall situation is desperate and has been created over many years. It will not be resolved overnight with short-term programmes or fads. An often quoted analogy for this kind of decline is 'boiling a frog'. If one throws a frog into boiling water it will jump out. To carry out this cruel task one puts the frog in cold water and gradually raises the temperature. The frog feels warm and comfortable and eventually falls asleep – permanently. The process is so slow it is not recognised. Many economies and communities are in this situation. They have not been 'fortunate' enough to have dramatic and obvious crises to face up to. Decline has only been noticed over many years.

It is worth investigating the vicious circle of decline in more detail. The underlying paradigms will be explored later. The process of decline is circular so it is possible to start at any point. Take the manufacturing sector, the powerhouse of any economy. In most Western economies it is subjected to unreasonable pressures for short-term dividend performance. As a consequence internal investment decisions are governed by very high internal rates of return. This acts as a disincentive to all forms of investment.

Manufacturing companies will tend to under-invest in people as well as in plant. This is guaranteed to lead to a decline in the quality of production processes and hence products and services. With poor skills and equipment, the costs of failure, such as scrap, rework, warranty, etc., will rise. In many manufacturing companies these costs can be as high as 25% of revenue! This is bound to lead to reduced long-term profitability but, more seriously, to the over-pricing of products and services as compared with competitors.

So the communities' businesses, through poor quality, are generating decreasing profits and eventually major losses. This creates a vicious circle within the businesses. That is, there is less to invest, particularly in education and training, and so staff have even less chance of learning new skills. As profitability is falling, wages fall in real terms over time, and eventually jobs are lost.

In the meantime government revenue is falling because companies and individuals have lower earnings to tax. Unemployment has a double edge because reducing revenue now has to be spent on increasing social security costs. As government revenue falls and social security costs rise there is less and less to invest nationally and locally on infrastructure such as roads, rail and computer networks and less on education and training, as well as health and security.

Declining infrastructure will reduce the communities' chances of attracting inward investment and reduce the quality and productivity of existing firms even more. Meanwhile, lower investment in schools, colleges and universities reduces the knowledge base and weakens future prospects for innovation and enterprise. Thus poorly equipped students leave education either to join the dole queues, or if they are lucky, to join an organisation. These new employees with find it difficult to cope unless they have real 'learning to learn' skills. As a consequence they are unlikely to be able to partake in continual improvement and the processes decline even more. This is where the vicious circle started.

Western economies and communities are not in healthy states and their decline is continuing generally unabated. What are the causes of this decline and how can it be halted and reversed?

Flawed Paradigms

The causes of the present problems are systemic. The real problem lies in the way in which organisations and economies are managed (2). All methods of management are based on certain principles or beliefs. These form prevalent paradigms. A paradigm is a set of rules and regulations (written or unwritten) that does two things. It establishes or defines boundaries and it tells you how to behave inside the boundaries in order to be successful (3).

The most powerful paradigms are those that are never questioned or challenged. A paradigm shift (4) occurs when someone sees something from a very different angle. Paradigm shifters do not have easy lives. They tend to question and challenge and are usually on the fringe of the establishment. Those who invested most in an existing paradigm are likely to be the last to leave it. How a community treats its mavericks is likely to strongly influence its ability to innovate and to move on. Large organisations have, historically, not been good places for innovative people. In Britain it is the 'solid players' that get promoted. Most highly innovative people find corporate cultures stifling and tend to get out at the earliest possible moment.

Values and principles have a profound impact on all human actions. In fact there is no such thing as value-free human behaviour. Every person has a world view (5). This defines how they answer fundamental questions about why they exist, what the problems are and how they can be resolved. Christians have a very clearly defined world view but so do atheists, humanists and even nihilists. In order to make progress people and organisations need to examine their underlying world views. Only then will they be able to question paradigms and develop more appropriate means of tackling prevalent problems.

So what are some of the current Western paradigms that prevent the development of new solutions to the existing problems?

1 Market Forces can resolve Everything

The Eighties saw the emergence of a seductive but naive view that market forces were in some way 'natural' and that they should not be challenged. The only way to improve an economy was to free markets from state intervention and to let them operate as they wished, despite the social consequences. It is fair to say that in Britain, prior to Margaret Thatcher's election; centralist socialism had certainly shown itself to be woefully lacking in effective solutions. Many organisations such as British Telecom, British Airways and the then British Leyland needed to be released from slow bureaucratic control to attempt to compete more globally. But equally so organisations such as the Royal Mail have shown that you do not need to be in the private sector to improve your performance dramatically.

Markets are human constructed. They have no divine right to go unchallenged. They have to be considered in their social and political contexts. Privatisation went from being an appropriate approach for certain organisations to becoming a political dogma, or paradigm, that was beyond challenge. The conclusion of this is the creation of two or three-tier systems in health and education, greater inequality and social dysfunction, along with enormous bureaucracies to manage 'internal markets'. There is enough evidence to show that, with good quality leadership and appropriate checks and balances, public sector organisations can do just as good a job as their private sector counterparts in very complex and subtle environments. *Market forces are not the only means of improving the performance of organisations.*

2   Competition is Always good

Markets are supposed to be efficient because they are based on competition. The concept of competition has been taken to its extreme. Many organisations actively encourage competition within. Very simple exercises based on game theory can be used to show how, if every part of an organisation is encouraged to maximise its own gain, this can do great harm to the whole. This is called sub-optimisation. Barings Bank is a fine example of the damage that can be done when traders are encouraged to compete ruthlessly.

Sub-optimisation does not just occur within organisations. It often occurs across whole systems of organisations. Time after time it has been shown that it is often better for one part of a system to take a loss for the greater good. This is unlikely to happen where competition is endemic. Japanese firms have taken co-operation to interesting limits, in some cases intervening to assist competitors that are in trouble and certainly supporting suppliers. The key is to define the system. *Once the system is defined encourage co-operation not competition within the boundaries.*

3   If it ain't broke don't fix It

This commonly heard phrase has done incredible damage to British industry. It legitimised complacency and ignorance. Many organisations in the West focus on problem solving, putting right something that has gone wrong. They need to do far more than this. You do not have to be ill to get healthier. Continual, never ending improvement, necessary for survival, is far more than just problem solving. Whilst Western firms were busy fixing things the Japanese were busy working on the real problem: variation. They realised that every product, service or process can be improved and the key was to reduce variation and hence minimise the loss to society of the production of the product or service.

Critical to improvement is knowing why something works. This involves experimentation and a short-term interruption for a longer-term gain. Maybe it is the inherent short-termism of many Western organisations that encouraged this paradigm to be accepted. Another factor is the amount of fear in organisations. If one is going to try to improve a process this means taking risks, which always means failure at some point. 'Failing forward' is inevitable in improvement. In fearful environments people will not take risks and stagnation will be the result. *If it ain't broke, investigate it and find a way of improving it.*

4   People need to be motivated

One view of a manager's role is that he or she is there to motivate. Another, but very different view, is that a manager exists to remove the barriers to motivation. One reason why the latter statement makes far more sense is that the majority of the root causes of problems or issues come from the system not the individual. If the individual is not empowered and supported to make improvements there is little he or she can do. Motivation schemes seem to take little account of this fact. They also tend not to take into account that people are all different with different wants and needs. In the old South Africa all the answers to questions were 'white'. They took no account of cultural diversity and many motivation schemes failed to work as a result. What might motivate a white middle-class male is unlikely to motivate a black woman.

There is another reason why motivation schemes are often flawed. They are designed on the premise that people need external motivation. Every human being is born with incredible internal motivation. You don't have to force a child to love learning; they are born that way. Unfortunately right from the first moments of life they are exposed to the 'forces of destruction' (6) that drive out these wonderful intrinsic desires. These forces include grading and ranking, win/lose educational systems, excessively ambitious parents, merit schemes at school and finally, employers finish the job off with 'employee of the month' schemes, league tables and individual performance-related pay. *People are inherently motivated; they do need others trying to make them so. Work on removing the barriers instead.*

5   Only manage what you can measure

A recent Royal Society for the encouragement of the Arts (RSA) inquiry leading industrialists into the form of 'Tomorrow's Company' (7) has concluded that a major barrier to success has been the over reliance on financial measures. Dr Deming in *Out of the Crisis* (8) goes further, and refers to managing by visible figures alone as a Western deadly disease. Dr Nelson's now famous quote from *Out of the Crisis* is that 'the most important information for management is unknown and unknowable'.

Unfortunately many governments around the world, in their attempts to get more outputs from declining budgets, have introduced bureaucratic measurement regimes. Sadly it is true that 'what gets measured gets done'. Add this to Dr Nelson's conclusion and one gets a depressing overall conclusion that most energy gets expended on the less critical issues. *Aspire to measure using both quantitative and qualitative means but accept that ultimately some things will not be measured without trivialising them.*

6   Rights without Responsibilities

As Etzioni states in his book *The Spirit of Community* 'to take and not to give is an amoral, self-centred predisposition that ultimately no society can tolerate' (9). Much has been achieved by human rights organisations in the last 20/30 years but it is important to recognise that responsibilities go with rights. This is particularly true in stakeholding.

Shareholders have to accept that, if they are going to achieve reasonable long-term returns on their investments, they have certain responsibilities to the organisations in which they invest. Employees, if they expect to be actively involved in decision making, need to commit to the organisation and be willing to improve their own skills so that they can be involved effectively. Organisations that want to be 'approved suppliers' will have to realise that they need to commit resources and be prepared to put their customers' interests over their own from time to time. Students must accept responsibility for their own learning in return for much greater involvement in improving learning processes. The examples could go on for pages *but if you want rights you are going to have to take responsibilities.*

Drivers for Stakeholding

There are many reasons why the subject of stakeholding is on the agenda of most organisations. The precise reasons will vary from organisation to organisation but there do appear to be some common 'drivers' for change.

The first is probably overarching, and that is the need to improve effectiveness as well as efficiency. Most organisations have realised that the old tried and tested methods of management no longer seem to be delivering adequate results. They are searching for alternative approaches and many of these such as Total Quality seem to have stakeholding at their core. In fact Dr Deming proposed that the very purpose of any organisation was for everybody to gain – stockholders, employees, suppliers, customers, community, the environment – over the long-term (10). Disillusionment with traditional methods is one reason, but there are subsidiary ones.

Phenomenal rates of change is another reason that traditional methods are not working. Everyone is aware of the rate of change of technology. If you know about a certain technology, the likelihood is that it is 'old hat'. However, most other aspects of our world have been changing just as fast but less visibly.

Political environments have become less stable. The old demarcations between left and right have become blurred. Politicians seem just as unsure which way to turn as the general electorate. They are worried that some of the inevitable changes are election losers. Who would win an election advocating major reductions in state pension provision or restrictions in the use of the motor car? A major political driver for stakeholding in the public sector is the need to get more from less, due to ever decreasing budgets.

Economic conditions have been changing too. Global markets and the liquidity of international funds mean that circumstances can change rapidly, creating great turbulence for economies. In a recent workshop with professionals from a construction company, when asked to identify the biggest potential influence on their business they identified the economic impact of a possible withdrawal of the UK from the European Union. Overall the threats seemed to outweigh the benefits. Similarly nations seem to be divided on the issue of a European currency but if it occurs the changes will be profound.

Social conditions have been changing rapidly too. One hundred years ago Britain had four or five major belief systems, mostly derivatives of Christianity. Now there is much greater diversity and we are moving to a situation where each individual's belief system will be a unique hybrid of many. These changes are having profound effects on organisations as they try to adapt to spiritual diversity as well as other types of diversity. Changes in the construction of family units are presenting challenges as well as many other social factors. Throughout all of these social changes people have become more confident, with higher expectations and they are less willing to be placid receivers of service. This is a major reason to try to engage them directly.

Politics, economics, technology and social conditions are changing rapidly. Embracing stakeholding provides a means of trying to manage ever-increasing complexity in a turbulent world.

Chapter 2

What is Stakeholding?

Stakeholding is not a new concept. It recently become fashionable when New Labour developed their vision of a 'stakeholder society' for Britain. The political ideas have been borrowed mainly from the developed and co-ordinated economies of northern Europe, particularly Germany. At a micro-economic level the stakeholder revolution has been going on in organisations for the last ten or 15 years driven by initiatives such as Total Quality. The RSA inquiry into Tomorrow's Company assumes stakeholding as a central tenet of a vanguard organisation. They do, however, conclude that 'only by giving weight to the interests of all key stakeholders can shareholders' continuing value be assured' (11). Thus, according to the RSA, the main driver is still the shareholder and they believe that businesses can convince the financial community to provide longer-term support. Others, such as Will Hutton, would challenge this assumption. He proposes legislation to curb short-termism. What is apparent is that many people are using the term stakeholder without shared definitions. It is starting to mean very different things to different people.

Definitions

Before attempting to define the terms it is important to recognise that the current debates seem to be focusing on two levels of stakeholding – the macro, or political, and the micro, or organisational. The former concentrates on legislation and nationwide political and social structures. The latter, the greater focus of this book, focuses on what all types of organisations are able to do in order to improve their own performance.

At any level one can only start to make sense of stakeholding when it is related to specific political, social or organisational processes. The subject of process management has come of age and will be explored in much greater detail later in the book. Some of the basic principles need to be reviewed before giving definitions of stakeholders and stakeholding.

People often use the term 'system' interchangeably with 'process'. Dr Deming defined a system as 'a network of interdependent components that work together to accomplish the aim of the system' (12). If there is no shared aim there is no system, just activities. An alternative definition is that a process is a series of inter-linked activities, which transform inputs from suppliers into outputs for customers, utilising both human and physical resources and operating under some form of control. This can be represented pictorially (Figure 1).

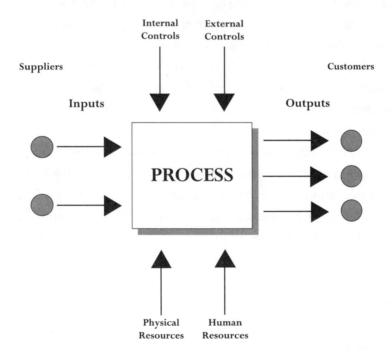

Figure 1. Diagrammatic view of a Process

To start to understand a process of any kind one needs to define its boundaries. This is agreeing what is 'in the box' and what is outside. Processes cut through organisations and communities. Government, industry, education and the voluntary sector are inextricably linked together in complex processes.

Defining the process helps to identify the customers, those people who receive the outputs from the process. The term customer, as used here, does not necessarily imply any financial transaction, and customers can be both internal and external to the organisation. In fact, in communities the main components are customers and suppliers of each other. For example, industry might supply both education and government with goods and services. Government in turn provides safe, reliable infrastructure for industry and education. Education supplies responsible, well-educated citizens to take up fulfilling roles in organisations of all types. The voluntary sector provides high quality services to both government and education whilst receiving funds from the former. In this way all the organisations are linked together, as customers and suppliers, to provide a high quality of life for all the citizens.

Processes can be analysed at any level. A community can be regarded as comprising many high-level core processes. Alternatively, within manufacturing, the new product development process could be reviewed. At the other extreme every small activity, like writing a memo, could be regarded as a process.

So returning to stakeholding, stakeholders can only be defined in their relationship to a process. A stakeholder is a person, or group of persons, who has an interest or concern in a particular process resulting from some direct or indirect involvement. Stakeholding is a process by which stakeholders are actively involved in the design, delivery, review and improvement of products and services, including political and social services, in order to ensure that all gain over the long term.

Stakeholders include customers, suppliers, employees, owners and other providers of capital, regulators and interest groups. A useful way to classify stakeholders is to divide them into four categories: customers, controllers, partners and the core.

Charles Handy defines the core as those people that are essential to the organisation or process (13). The core includes key staff including professionals, managers and owner-managers.

Partners are not in the core. They are the people through whom part or all of the service is provided, as well as suppliers of goods and services. Partners include traditional suppliers, sub-contractors, distributors, agents, franchisees, consultants and part-time or temporary staff.

Controllers define, regulate and influence the organisation or process. Controllers include regulators, legislators, providers of capital including funders of voluntary and government services, the media and trustees.

Customers are those people who receive the product or service. Some customers receive it directly. They are primary customers, the people for whom the original product or service was designed. Secondary customers receive the service indirectly, 'downstream' of the primary customers. Secondary customers include the relatives of primary customers, the broader community and interest groups representing the environment. All of these people are stakeholders at one time or another.

Stakeholding is successful when all stakeholders gain over the long term. It is about aiming for a truly sustainable win/win/win/etc., situation. It is not as easy as it might sound and there are many potential pitfalls for the unwary. Satisfying stakeholders over the long term is not just about giving them what they ask for. It is about ensuring that both their wants and needs are met and sometimes even exceeded. The key to this is close dialogue and careful management of expectations.

The definitions in this section have proven useful over the last ten years. They can never be definitive and people interested in stakeholding are encouraged to use them and modify them accordingly. They will, however, be referred to in the rest of this book, so that author and reader have some workable definitions.

Underpinning Principles

In the first chapter flawed paradigms were highlighted. Alternatives need to be developed to replace these ways of thinking. Many 'gurus' have espoused their prescriptions for successful organisations and communities. All models are inherently limited and no list of principles can be totally complete. In this section a distillation of many of these ideas is presented around four fundamental principles.

1 Co-operation

All stakeholders can only gain in the long-term if all transactions are based on high levels of co-operation. Co-operation has to be founded on trust and trustworthiness (14). Trust takes years to build up and can be weakened, or even destroyed, very quickly and easily. It is impossible to put a value on trust, yet it is core to the success of all endeavours. Trust can only be built by people being open and honest with each other. Before stakeholders can enter into any meaningful partnerships they need to start to understand each other's wants and needs and each other's 'worlds'. Hidden agendas can profoundly undermine trust but it is too naive to expect potential partners to disclose their positions immediately. There is no short cut and it will take time. Ignoring this mutual understanding may lead to the appearance of rapid progress but will ultimately lead to problems. Stakeholding inevitably has to be 'slow to be fast' (15). John Carlisle in his book *Beyond Negotiation* (16) defines discreet stages that stakeholder teams need to go through to achieve their tasks. Preparation cannot be bypassed.

Fear is like a cancer to effective partnerships. It undermines trust and must be actively driven out (17). This is easier said than done. Fear, like entropy, creeps into all processes. Different people are fearful of different things. Once again open and honest communication is the way to identify the fears and to start to remove the causes, or at least to minimise them. A very useful technique is to get teams of stakeholders to define and agree their own 'code of co-operation'. This can be documented and acts as a 'contract' between all the parties.

When the team of stakeholders is secure enough they can start to agree a common aim or purpose. Without constancy of purpose (18) there can only be confusion and even more turbulence than necessary. Constancy of purpose is not about Vision and Mission Statements on the walls. It is what is in people's 'hearts and minds'. Creating a common purpose must be a collective process involving all stakeholders.

Building co-operation based on trust is not an event, it is a continuous process. However without it the other principles, methods and tools of stakeholding are unlikely to succeed.

2 Continual Improvement

Continual improvement is a mindset. It is very different to concepts of conformance. It is based on the premise that there is no such thing as a perfect process. All processes can be improved indefinitely. Whether a process is a priority for improvement is another matter. Western approaches to management have tended to concentrate on conformance to agreed standards. If the product or service falls between certain tolerances then it is good, if not it is bad. This is very 'digital', or black and white, thinking. The world, contrary to what the electronics industries say, is in fact very 'analogue', with variation everywhere. The goal is to reduce variation and ensure that the loss to society (19) as a whole is minimised. It is not enough to say 'are we meeting this standard?' Organisations and communities must concentrate on raising the standards.

Continual improvement is concerned with dealing with root causes not symptoms. Too much of what is done is done in business, political and social arenas is simply responding to immediate demands without getting to the heart of the issues. Root causes tend to be miles away in distance and time from the symptom (20). This means that whilst the symptom may be experienced in one part of the system or process, the real roots could be much further 'upstream', often in other organisations. The only way to continually improve organisations and communities is to actively engage all the stakeholders in the improving of processes. This minimises the risk of 'window-dressing'.

Continual improvement can only be truly effective if it is founded on sound theories of learning. Much progress has been made in this area over the last 20 years. Human understanding of the processes of learning, whilst still relatively in its infancy, is becoming more sophisticated. We are starting to understand different intelligences, learning styles, levels of learning and how to improve and speed up learning. Stakeholder groups can be very diverse and many people may not have had academic training. They are still able to learn and make powerful contributions as long as those guiding or facilitating the continual improvement process work on removing the barriers to learning.

3   Inclusiveness

If organisations and communities are going to engage stakeholders they must work on removing the barriers to inclusiveness. The statement that 'we are all different' is almost too trite to mention. We would probably all agree with it but how many of us act on this belief? There are often wide gaps between belief and action and this gap concerned diversity is very pronounced. In the Monty Python film the *Life of Brian*, Brian, who has been mistaken for the Messiah, is speaking to a large crowd that is following him. He opens his window to find them all waiting on his every word. He says to them that they are all individuals and they respond in unison, 'yes, we are all individuals'. This is how organisations and communities treat people. Do we really celebrate diversity or is it an inconvenience?

The barriers to inclusiveness are often built into systems and processes at the design stage. Appraisal processes are a good example. Often these are inflexible and precisely defined. They may work well for the benefit of the prevailing social group, usually white middle-class males. How do people from ethnic minorities fare in this process? Often they are blamed for under-performing when the real problem lies with the process. Recruitment processes are often another example of systemic discrimination. Why are all the answers to questions white? Even one particular stakeholder group is very diverse. How are gender, racial, sexual, physical and age diversity to be encouraged? A quality organisation or community is one that practices equality of opportunity (21).

Just incorporating stakeholding into an organisation's Mission Statement is unlikely to make any real difference unless the organisation takes proactive steps to include the different groups. Opening up access for people in the *core* will take a lot more than rhetoric. Lack of participation is often caused by a lack of investment in training and education and by hierarchical management structures. Insecurity is a key constraint. Unfortunately few organisations have the courage to drive out fear by providing job security. Most are systematically reducing security. Land Rover is an exception with its 'New Deal' for core staff. This guarantees employment as long as people are prepared to be flexible. If improvements make jobs redundant the company will take on the responsibility for providing retraining for a new role. The employee needs to be willing to learn. This has lead to a great increase in staff suggestions and is a good example of rights with responsibilities. No one can make someone learn – that ultimately is their responsibility – but organisations can do a lot to encourage staff to learn.

Including *partners* in much deeper, long-term relationships is well established in industry. Unfortunately in the public sector Compulsory Competitive Tendering (CCT) often mandates against these kinds of partnerships. 'Blue Chip' companies have been systematically reducing their supplier bases for many years. It is impossible to have a deep relationship with thousands of suppliers. However, selecting which organisations will become preferred suppliers requires a thorough process that covers much more than costs of goods and services. The aim is to minimise the total cost of a supply, not the purchase cost. Good selection processes cover how well the supplier works with its stakeholders, its long-term strategy and how it continually improves its processes, as well as how it invests in staff. Relationships with partners should be based on joint working, open-book accounting, good communication and high levels of trust. It is not untypical for a customer to provide support to preferred suppliers that find themselves in temporary difficulty. It makes sound financial sense. Sadly in the UK 73% of middle-size companies disagree that they should operate in partnership with their larger customers, instead preferring to maintain adversarial commercial relationships. Who said the private sector has got all of the answers?

Incorporating *controllers* such as investors, and other providers of funds, is more problematic. These stakeholders often take a very 'hands off' approach, demanding high returns or high performance levels without much of a reciprocal commitment. Relationships with controllers can create a lot of conflict and resentment, which actually weakens both parties' positions. This problem is often seen in government agencies or quangos (quasi-autonomous non-governmental organisations). Civil servants are often unwilling to enter into closer relationships, often preferring to 'dictate' performance from their offices. These barriers need to be broken down and this requires movement from both sides. Best practice involves including controllers in strategic planning. If this is impractical then the very least one can do is to communicate strategic intent, not just focusing on financial issues, but including a much broader range of indicators. The key is open, honest, two-way communication. It pays off in the long run.

Some people believe that these changes can be brought about from the 'bottom up'. Others believe government intervention and legislation is required before particular investors will change their behaviour. It is unlikely that any government will have the confidence to tackle the City and global markets, even if they could. One myth that needs dispelling in the private sector is that directors have legally to concentrate on pleasing current shareholders even if this is at the expense of the long-term health of the enterprise. Directors have a duty to the company, not any third party. According to the RSA inquiry there is nothing to stop directors giving regard to other stakeholders' interests if they judge in good faith that this will benefit the health of the company.

There are many tried and tested ways of engaging *Customers* in organisations. The more traditional methods, such as market research, involve less direct contact but can involve large numbers. Other methods include getting customers directly involved in strategic planning and improvement activities and customer clinics. These methods may not be so statistically valid but they encourage other stakeholders to understand the customers. Other ways of keeping close to customers include observing customers, sending staff on placement and secondments with customers and being the customer. One Hospital Trust chief executive decided to pretend to be a patient in his own organisation. This revealed far more than many of the more formal methods. An Ambulance Trust director keeps close to customers by spending a shift in an ambulance, with the paramedics, at least once every two weeks. This has improved morale tremendously and led to many improvements. Customers usually do not instigate innovations to service and products but, by keeping close to them, it encourages all other stakeholders to come up with ideas. If you believe that the people you serve are important, show it in your behaviour. You will be surprised.

4   Systems Thinking

Systems thinking is so central to effective stakeholding that Chapter 3 is dedicated to the subject. Some of the key principles are summarised here. Understanding system or process is one way to identify stakeholders. A system without a shared aim isn't really a system at all. Systems exist to ensure that all stakeholders receive long-term benefits. Competition within systems is generally destructive and can lead to sub-optimisation with everyone 'fighting their own corner' and ignoring the bigger picture. Measurement must be based on sound theory or it can do more harm than good. Stakeholders should be actively involved in establishing measures and goals. Don't measure what is easy, start with what is important, bearing in mind that some of the most important information is unknown or unknowable.

Multiple Relationships

People do not usually fit conveniently into one stakeholder category. In the case of a privatised utility many customers are shareholders too. Large numbers of staff own shares and they are all customers of the organisation. In a school a parent may also be a governor and be involved in running a local business. Most users of public services are at the same time taxpayers. Typically as stakeholders we have several different types of relationship with an organisation at one time. A useful way to picture this is with a Venn diagram (Figure 2).

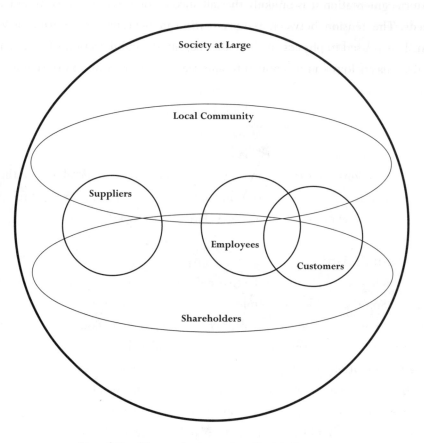

Figure 2. Venn Diagram showing overlap of Stakeholder categories

Win/win theory is seductively straightforward. In reality its application is a great deal more complex. Firstly stakeholder groups may not be homogeneous. Every stakeholder is an individual with specific expectations. Organisations have to consider collective wants and needs. Segmentation of stakeholders, as with market segmentation, has to be done carefully and needs to be research based. Segmentation might be done on age, ethnicity, geography, gender, etc.

Consensus and Prioritisation

Even after segmentation it is unlikely that all stakeholders will share common wants and needs. The tension between requirements can be represented using a Vector diagram. This is used in physics to show the magnitude and direction of forces acting on a body. This analogy can be applied to an organisation or community (Figure 3).

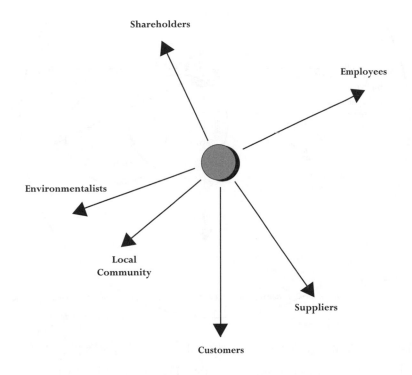

Figure 3. Vector Diagram showing differing Stakeholder requirements

Consider a school. The governors may want the school to offer a broad education to the whole of the local community. The department of education may have a political agenda to reintroduce selective education, to measure success solely in terms of academic performance and to do it as cheaply as possible. Parents may be more concerned about the physical and mental safety and security of their children. Pupils put a lot of emphasis on securing employment, while employers are looking for self-motivated team players who can help them innovate and improve (Figure 4).

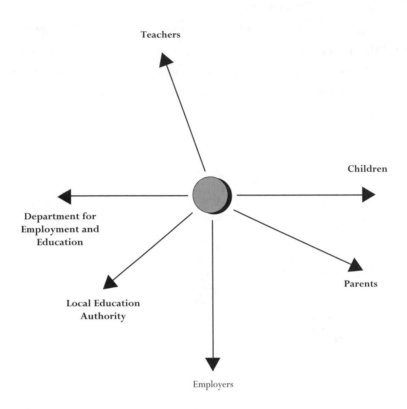

Figure 4. Vector Diagram showing differing Stakeholder requirements for a school

Leaders must aspire to meet and exceed all of the wants and needs of all of the stakeholders. In reality this may not be possible. They are faced with some challenges. Firstly they must look for the common ground. This can only be done by bringing the parties together and starting facilitated dialogues to break down the barriers, including prejudices and stereotypes. Many people involved in these types of sessions are encouraged by the fact that they have more in common than they thought. They also start to appreciate each other's positions and difficulties. In this scenario leaders are trying to facilitate the different parties to start pulling in the same overall direction (Figure 5).

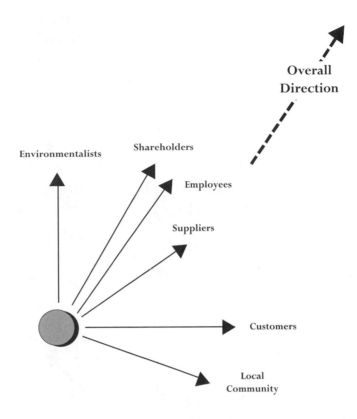

Figure 5.Vector Diagram showing alignment of Stakeholder's requirements

If consensus is difficult to achieve then leaders may have to take a different approach, prioritising particular stakeholders. In many cases this should not be necessary. In the case of a private company the best way to provide long-term high dividends is to delight customers by having highly motivated core staff and partners and by being seen as a responsible firm in the community. Sometimes the gaps are too difficult to bridge and leaders and other stakeholders need to take tough decisions (Figure 6).

An example of this has occurred in the Training and Enterprise Council (TEC) movement in the UK. TECs are quangos funded by the Department of Education and Employment, the main controller, to provide a wide range of services to promote local prosperity. They provide programmes to young people, unemployed people, people with special needs and employers themselves. These are the primary customers. There are 80 TECs across England and Wales. The cultures vary quite dramatically. At one end of the spectrum are those TECs that see themselves as extensions of the Civil Service. Their main priority is to serve the Department, and thus will concentrate on short-term targets and goals at all cost. At the other end are the TECs whose priority is to put their primary customers first. To them all that counts is making a real difference for local people and they will tend to ignore some of the pressures from the Civil Servants. In reality no TEC can exist at the extremes, they will lose the support of one of the two stakeholder groups. Many have worked hard to build a closer partnership with the controller while still putting the community first. It has been a difficult and frustrating challenge.

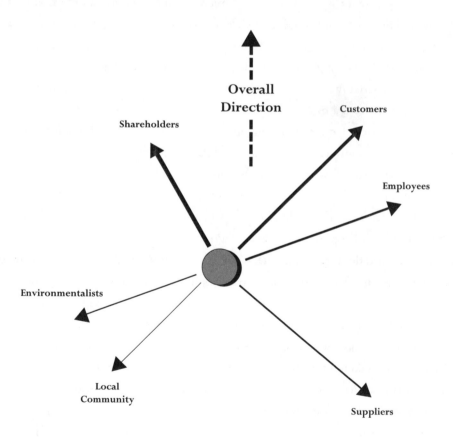

Figure 6. Vector Diagram showing prioritisation of Stakeholder requirements

These two responses to conflicts of requirements, building consensus and prioritising, are not alternatives. It might be necessary to prioritise for a period of years whilst working to break down the barriers with other groups. Ultimately consensus can be the only successful strategy.

Levels of Stake

Not all stakeholders have the same level of stake in a process. The level of concern or interest can vary from very low to very high. If there is no concern or interest then the person, or persons, cannot be called a stakeholder. The level will directly affect the groups' commitment to becoming engaged in the process. Consider some examples.

An owner-manager is likely to have a much greater stake in an organisation than a pension fund holder is, unless company law or attitudes change greatly in the next few years. A person who has highly desirable, transferable skills and knowledge may well have a lower stake than a person who does not. An example of this is a consultant in a hospital. Alternatively someone who has been encouraged to develop by an organisation may have a high stake based on loyalty. A supplier who has high demand for goods or services from a wide customer base may be more reluctant to enter into a comprehensive supplier partnership with a customer than one who provides a specialist service to a few customers. Business consultants often have high stakes in their client organisations because their reputations will be linked to the client's success. A customer who is highly dependent on a product or service and does not have much choice of supplier may have a high stake. For example, someone on Income Support is highly dependent on the Benefits Agency to make correct payments on time. They have no choice of alternative supplier and their welfare depends on the service. Alternatively, someone forced onto a government training scheme to ensure receipt of benefits may feel uncommitted and think that they have a low stake.

The level of stake depends on specific circumstances but is influenced by the importance the stakeholder attaches to the wants and needs they have of the process, the alternatives available to them and personal factors such as loyalty, sense of duty, self-esteem and personal aspirations.

Chapter 3

Understanding the System

Western Reductionism

Western thinking has tended to concentrate on analytical skills, based on dissection. Subjects are broken down into their component parts, each part is analysed in depth and new specialisations emerge. This is often necessary in managing complexity but there are inherent dangers. A motorcycle can be analysed in many ways (24). At one level it comprises a fuel delivery system, a combustion engine, a transmission system, a suspension system, a lighting system, etc. Any of these systems could be broken down into lower level components. There is a danger, when one gets down into the lowest levels, that one misses interdependencies and their overall purpose which is to enable fast and reliable transportation. As a whole, the machine takes on a sense of identity and even beauty.

This specialisation has been taken to extremes in secondary education. Each subject is compartmentalised to the extent that students miss inter-relationships and universal subjects, like learning to learn, and are often excluded altogether because they don't fit neatly into a subject category. Many years ago the BBC produced a programme called *Burke's Connections*. The presenter, James Burke, would start the programme with a piece of knowledge from one discipline and period of history and then during the course of a half-hour show all the connections that led to a completely different subject in space and time. Most people would never have dreamt that the subjects were linked.

Mt. Edgecumbe High School in Sitka, Alaska, is world renowned for the transformation that the stakeholders have achieved. This school regularly uses cross-curricular projects to bring depth and interest to learning. One famous example was an entrepreneurial class project that was based on producing smoked salmon for Japanese consumers. The project started with investigating smoking techniques (Technology/Food Science) and their impacts on Salmon flesh (Science). The students realised they needed to understand much more about the consumers' customs and practices (History/Social Studies). Packaging had to be designed (Art) and certain information needed to be written in Japanese (Foreign Language). All the way through the project students were deciding on production, distribution and financial issues (Business). Finally all their findings and experiences had to be documented in one report (English). They developed many other skills including team working, planning and time management. There was wholeness to the learning experience, which made it far more effective than traditional methods.

This tendency to compartmentalise is endemic in Western organisations and communities. Systems' thinking is a very different way of viewing the world and is an alternative to the pervasive reductionism in Western culture.

Command and Control

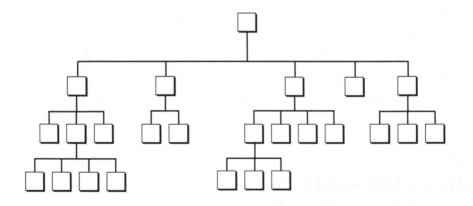

Figure 7. Tree Diagram showing traditional hierarchy of organisations

When people are asked to show how their organisation operates they often draw a top to bottom tree diagram (Figure 7). This kind of structure goes back a long way in history. One of the earliest documented references is in the Book of Exodus. However, it is a singularly one-dimensional view and can be representative of some very outdated thinking. This kind of tree diagram only shows who is accountable to whom in the structure. It does not show how work gets done. The premise behind this model is one of 'command and control'. The role of management is get their ideas into the hands of the workers and then check up on how well they have implemented these ideas. The people at the top of the structure have 'big heads and little hands' whilst the people at the bottom have 'big hands and little heads'. This is blatant nonsense but the remnants of this way of thinking can still be seen in many organisations and projects.

Some of the common attributes of hierarchical organisations are as follows:

- Highly departmental.
- Poor communications.
- Low trust and high blame.
- 'Boss' is seen as most important 'customer'.
- Slow to respond to change.
- Success measured in size of 'empire'.
- Information is seen as power and protected.
- Little initiative.
- Top heavy.

Even the most established and traditional 'command and control' organisations, such as the army and the police, are now looking at more responsive and empowering ways of managing. 'Command and control' certainly worked in its time but there is a very different paradigm.

Process Organisations

Some of the basic concepts of process have already been covered. They need to be explored in more detail along with complementary concepts such as measurement theory. (The terms *process* and *system* are being used interchangeably in this book.)

A process is a series of inter-linked activities which transform inputs from suppliers into outputs for customers, utilising both human and physical resources and operating under some form of control (see Figure 1). Processes cut across organisations and communities. A more representative diagram of an organisation is shown in Figure 8.

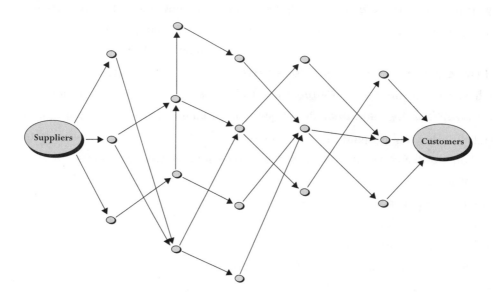

Figure 8. The 'Bird's Nest' of Processes

Some of the common attributes of process organisations are as follows:

- Minimal hierarchy.
- Improving communications.
- High trust and low blame.
- Focused on external and internal customers.
- Rapid to respond to change.
- Success measured in impact on customers.
- Information is widely distributed.
- Highly empowering.
- 'Flat' with few middle levels.

Functions and organisations are inextricably linked together in customer/supplier chains. One of the roles of a leader is to facilitate stakeholders to work on the bigger system making sure that it is optimised. Leaders have to have a 'mountain top' view of processes. The majority of the root causes of problems come from the very process itself so it is futile to exhort people to try harder or do better. The leader has to ensure that all stakeholders have the right skills and environment to be put to work on improving the process.

The Community as a System

Maybe one of the biggest challenges today is to try to understand communities as systems. This is taking one of the highest-level views possible and will engage all stakeholders. Firstly community needs to be defined. The term, like stakeholding, is used widely but it means different things to different people. What is a community? A community exists where there are common interests that unite people. These may be based on:

- personal attributes, such as race, age, gender, sexuality, etc.
- personal belief systems including religion, political views, etc.
- economic status or activity such as unemployment.
- knowledge or skill such as professions, trades, etc.
- relationship to a particular service i.e., a customer group such as residents, students, etc.
- geography or location (26).

At any point in our lives we are part of many diverse communities. Community spirit, however, only exists when there is a feeling of belonging to a community, expressed in mutual support (27). Humans are communal beings. If we cannot relate to socially acceptable communities then we will create less desirable ones, like street gangs. One of the reasons for introducing stakeholding concepts is to start to work on the barriers that exclude so many people from equitable and full participation in positive communities.

Any attempt to show how a community functions as a system is bound to involve simplification. The following is an attempt to identify the main elements and to show, in overview, how they inter-relate. Many linkages have been left out for clarity. Figure 9 diagrammatically represents what is explained in the following text. It shows how all the components need to concentrate on improvement to provide a high quality of life under a common purpose. Details will vary according to the social, economic and political environment of the community being considered. This model is based on British institutions and is not put forward as an example of how things should be, rather as how they are now. Each main component of the community will be considered in turn.

In the UK, Parliament and the European Union own the main processes for generating legislation that then defines and regulates all other parts of the system. Other bodies, such as the British Standards Institute, government departments and local authorities, produce standards and guidelines which again guide parts of the system. These organisations also have a responsibility for facilitating, with the rest of the community, the generation of long-term strategy. This helps to create constancy for the community and ensures that subsequent activities align to a greater purpose.

Once the strategy and policies are clear, within a legislative framework, priorities for funding can be established. The Inland Revenue and Customs & Excise are responsible for collecting revenue from individuals and organisations, but the Treasury controls its distribution. Once central government and the Treasury have decided on overall allocations many other bodies such as local authorities, and an ever-increasing number of quangos decide on more detailed funding priorities. Charities redistribute wealth less formally. The recently introduced National Lottery is another vehicle for this process.

These funds are then used, often alongside private finance, to provide products and services to the community. The maintenance and improvement of the infrastructure provide the foundation of the community. This includes the provision of housing, transport systems and electronic infrastructure. These processes may be initiated by public bodies but will usually involve public/private partnerships. The infrastructure is not only used by the citizens, but also by all other community organisations such as schools and businesses. The infrastructure and environment have a very great impact on the overall quality of life.

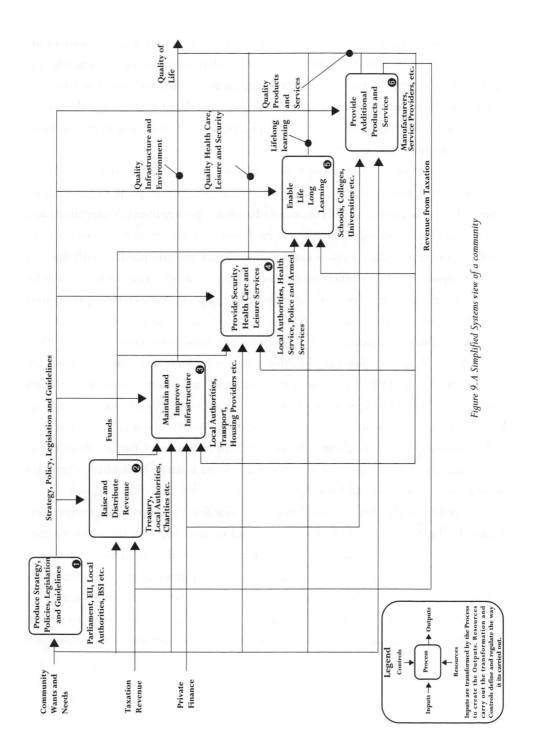

Figure 9. A Simplified Systems view of a community

Certain organisations are concerned with the provision of health care, leisure activities and ensuring that the community is safe. These include hospitals, leisure centres, the police, prisons and even the armed services. They depend on funds and products and services to ensure a safe and healthy community.

All community members should have equal access to life-long learning. Schools, colleges, universities and employers provide this opportunity. They are becoming more and more conscious about improving standards and reducing costs. They, like all the other organisations, can only do this in partnership with other community stakeholders. This process is likely to differentiate communities as they struggle to gain or retain the high value jobs.

Finally there is a raft of community businesses that provide products and services direct to the public and to other organisations in the system. They need to guarantee that they are continually improving their products and processes to ensure profitability and employment. By this means government is able to raise the revenue, so critical to keeping the system functioning and improving.

Whilst this is a simplification of an incredibly complex process and it misses out some components, it does illustrate the fact that all parts of the system are linked together and that the only way to achieve real improvement is to work together on the system.

The only way to ensure that quality of life improves for all the citizens is to ensure that the whole system works together. Competition within the system is likely to lead to conflict and short-termism. It is to be expected that some parts of the system will never be self-sufficient. Consider the transport system in Sheffield. The trams are clean, modern, reliable, safe and regular. They operate with subsidies but the overall benefits they bring to Sheffield are significant, though difficult to quantify. They include more rapid movement of residents and visitors, more efficient business, more inner city retailing, less congestion, less pollution and less tangible benefits such as better reputation and a greater pride in the city. Thus one part of the system, not driven to maximise profits, ensures that the overall system, the whole city, does better as a consequence. The challenge is to ensure continual improvement without competition. This requires talented leadership but the public sector is showing that, despite all the difficulties of low funding and low morale, it can be done.

Quality of Life

Measuring success of processes is an important issue and measurement theory will be explored in this chapter. Quality of life is one means of comparing communities. The term is familiar to all. However, without a shared definition it is meaningless (28).

Consider the following example. Who has, or had, a better quality of life, the current residents of Toronto or the native Dene Indians, prior to the arrival of the Europeans? By what method are we going to judge? If one considers the prevalent Western viewpoint, then a growing economy is all-important. Listening to the news and reading the papers very quickly gives an indication of how a community judges its success. But is wealth creation the key measure of quality of life? By this criterion the Dene Indians' communities would rank very low compared to Toronto. If the definition included crime levels, mental and physical health, community relationships, a sense of belonging, stewardship of the environment, then the result might be very different.

Any definition of quality of life will include economic indicators but should also include health, security, equity, environment and employment prospects to name but a few. Some of the most important information will be unknown or unknowable, but we need to restore some balance and see quality of life holistically.

Describing Process

Because systems thinking is so central to real transformation it has been a priority to develop techniques to enable stakeholders to understand existing processes as well as defining new or improved ones. It is important to choose appropriate techniques to use with the stakeholders. Factors affecting the choice include the complexity of the process being improved and the acceptability of the technique to the stakeholders. Unfortunately, generally the more complex the process the more complex the technique required to understand it. If stakeholders are not trained and supported well they may struggle with some of the techniques.

The Process Definition is one the most important core tools in process management. It is used to understand existing processes and to design new or improved processes. It ensures that processes are properly scoped and that customers' wants and needs are understood. It also assists in defining other influences on the process and thus helps the team manage complexity. It is a proforma based on the diagrammatic representation of a process in Figure 1.

Flowcharting is widely used to describe process. Flowcharts are used to show the sequence of steps, key decision points, alternative paths and feedback within a process. There are several different types of flowchart.

The simplest flowchart only uses three symbols. An input/output flowchart shows how key documents are received and passed on. The deployment flowchart is designed to show which stakeholders are involved in the various steps of the flowchart. The page is divided up into columns, one for each stakeholder. If an activity or decision involves a stakeholder it is drawn within their column. In this way the deployment flowchart winds its way down the page. If more than one stakeholder is involved the symbol is drawn across the necessary columns.

When dealing with lengthy processes, as is often the case, it is necessary to structure diagrams. Flowcharts can be structured but there are several other commonly used structured modelling techniques. These can prove difficult for people with little previous exposure to systems thinking. The Process Model, based on a technique developed by the United States Air Force called IDef0, is used to analyse complex processes by highlighting and structuring the activities that make up the overall process. Figure 9 is an IDef0 diagram. Another technique is Structured Systems Analysis Design Methodology (SSADM) but this is really for the experts.

All of these techniques have strengths and limitations. If they are to be beneficial they need to be used by a competent facilitator. The facilitator is not only an expert in the tools and techniques but is sensitive to the group's needs and can encourage everyone to participate. Using process techniques with groups of stakeholders can really improve understanding and can help generate ideas.

Measurement

Measurement is possibly one of the most controversial and misunderstood subjects of our time. It should come with a government health warning but most governments have not understood some of the basic principles themselves. Even many highly qualified professionals regularly provide evidence of being 'ill-numerate', or illiterate in the use of numbers. Stakeholders need to be trained and supported in the use of data otherwise they could create many pitfalls.

All organisations, partnerships and project teams should aspire to measure their performance and to use data to drive improvement. However, some of the most important information for management is unknown or unknowable. This led Dr Deming to conclude that one of the 'deadly diseases' in the West is managing by visible figures alone. Notice he was not saying 'don't use visible figures', but use them cautiously. Concentration on figures alone can promote short-termism and often does not lead to the best results for shareholders, let alone other stakeholders. Good leaders regularly manage things that they can't measure precisely. The idea that you can only manage what you can measure is fundamentally flawed.

Sadly it is true that what gets measured tends to get done. Accepting this, and the fact that some of the most important things cannot be measured, leads to a depressing conclusion that a lot of time is wasted on less important issues in all types of organisations and situations.

Operational Definitions

Which is the biggest airport in the world? There could be as many as ten different answers to this question based on up to 15 different definitions. Biggest could be defined by land mass, number of passengers, number of flights, revenue, length of runway, frequency of flights, etc. It comes as a shock to many people that there is no such thing as a true numerical value. A measure can only be generated from a definition. If the definition is useful and shared between customers and suppliers then it is referred to as an operational definition.

The Conservatives are right when they say that unemployment is 2.5 million. The Labour Party is right when they say that it is nearer five million. One definition is based on people actively seeking work. The other is based on people who could work. The political parties do not have an operational definition. One could argue that one definition is more just but that depends on your beliefs and political views. Comparisons with other nations are meaningless unless based on common definitions. Numerical data presented without definitions are at best of little value or at worst potentially dangerous.

Arbitrary Targets

Consider what happens when targets are set badly, particularly when they are set arbitrarily. People tend to achieve targets 'by hook or by crook', especially if their pay is linked to them. The easiest way is to manipulate the definition, much easier to do if the person setting the target is unclear about it in the first place. The definition of unemployment has been revised over 30 times since 1973 by civil servants under pressure from their political masters. It has only got higher or remained the same on three occasions. The lead for manipulating definitions is coming from the highest levels in our societies.

The second option for achieving an arbitrary target is potentially more damaging. The process itself can be manipulated to appear as if it has been improved. Production staff may be tempted to 'pass off' unfinished product, or even faulty product, in order to meet monthly production targets. The products might be finished later, risking introducing more errors and delaying delivery to the customers. The UK Government has put a lot of emphasis on waiting lists in the Health Service. No patient should wait more than two years for an operation. Hospitals have found very creative ways of achieving these targets, sometimes jeopardising other patients with priority needs. Some hospitals have unofficial waiting lists for waiting lists. The patient doesn't go on the monitored waiting list until certain bureaucratic requirements are met. Schools are suffering the same problems. Because of the emphasis on academic performance, in particular percentages of students achieving five A to C grades at GCSE, there is a temptation not to enter students who are unlikely to pass. In these cases the drive to achieve targets is to the detriment of the customers and other stakeholders. Manipulation of definitions and processes is endemic throughout the public and private sectors. The responsibility for this lies with those who set the targets, that is the leaders.

It is possible that the targets inspire stakeholders genuinely to improve a process but this is unlikely if the conditions for effective target setting are not present. Targets can be useful but they need to be used with care and understanding. The real aspiration is never ending improvement and leaders have to lead by example not with behaviourist exhortations. Measurement must be based on trust and openness otherwise 'games' will be played.

Variation

If stakeholders are going to use data correctly they need to understand the nature of variation. Western culture tends to operate 'digitally'. Products either conform (go) or non-conform (no go). Politicians represent the 'left' or the 'right'. Students are clever or not. Issues are secular or spiritual. This dualism is very constraining. In reality the world is full of variation and it is often more helpful to think of spectra. For example, people often think of themselves as practical or theoretical. However, a person who has no theoretical reference can never learn and a person who is purely practical will never get anything done. So at one end of the spectrum is the pure theorist and at the other end the pure pragmatist. Few people, if any, are at the extremes. Most of us lie on the spectrum between the extremes. Some may have a particular leaning, but to function we need a balance. The world is 'analogue', full of variation.

A very useful concept in understanding variation is the Taguchi Loss Function (33). This was originally developed for manufacturing but it has much broader applications. A loss function describes the losses that a system suffers from different values of some adjustable parameter (34). The loss function takes into account the total loss to society not just the loss to any single organisation. Taguchi fully embraced systems thinking in this concept. The costs can be rough and, because some of the most important losses may not be translated into financial terms, the loss function is often used purely conceptually, to encourage people to think about the whole system.

The best way to explore the loss function is with an example. Consider a person who has suffered a heart attack and requires emergency health care. The process starts by someone realising the person having the heart attack is in need of help. Someone may hopefully administer first aid whilst someone else calls the emergency services. The control room logs the call and dispatches an ambulance to the address given by the person calling. The ambulance travels through the city to the address. On arrival the paramedics will administer emergency care. Assuming the patient is still alive, they will be taken to the casualty department where they will receive further treatment. They will require inpatient health care and when discharged from hospital may well need further rehabilitation in the community with their General Practitioner and other agencies and charities. The process cuts across many parts of the community.

A key variable is the time it takes from the heart attack to get a suitably qualified paramedic to the patient. This will vary due to many reasons: the position of the ambulance when despatched, the road traffic, the weather, accessibility to the patient, etc. As delays occur there will be losses to society. Responding to heart attacks quickly is essential. As delays increase there will be risks that more harm occurs to the patient. The direct costs will include longer rehabilitation and, if the person is economically active, lost production. Ultimately it will result in a loss to society that is unreasonable to try to put into financial terms — the death of the person. So as the response time increases, so does the loss to society, exponentially.

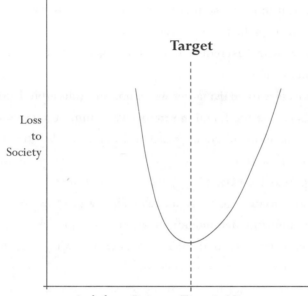

Figure 10. The Economic Loss Function for Ambulance response times

The ideal situation is to have a zero response time but as communities move to this point costs start to increase. It would be unreasonable to have a fully equipped ambulance on every street corner. The loss to society would be great because other public services would suffer as a result of the increased expenditure on health care. So with the current process the loss function might look like that shown in Figure 10.

It might not be possible to have thousands of ambulances but with a bit of creativity there may be ways of changing the process and hence the loss function to reduce response times dramatically. Some of the more obvious ways of improving the process include careful positioning of ambulances, using motorcycle paramedics, etc. The most innovative solution came from Seattle where they realised that an ambulance on each street was impractical but a trained citizen was not. They realised that the key measure was not the response time of the ambulance but the time it takes to get a qualified carer to the patient. Volunteers were requested for training, specifically in how to provide emergency care for heart attack victims. Several million people have received the training. Seattle is one of the best cities in which to have a heart attack because the chances are high that one of these volunteers will be nearby. By this imaginative approach Seattle has reduced the total losses to the community and ensured a higher quality of life.

The goal of any process is to be 'on target with minimum variation' (35). On target is defined in relationship to the minimum loss to society. Minimum variation means that all the outputs as are close to the target as possible. However, variation will still occur.

Common and Special Causes

There are two types of variation. Common causes are due to the process. They are inherent in the design, implementation and operation of the process. Common cause variation remains the same from day to day. Special causes, however, come from sources outside of the process. They relate to some special event. It is sensible to investigate the actual reason for the variation. It may be operator error, or extreme weather conditions, etc. In the ambulance example, common causes of variation would include traffic conditions, distance to scene and call handling procedures. Special causes could include ambulances being involved in accidents and errors in taking accident details.

The majority of problems belong to the system and are not the fault of individuals. Experience suggests that as many as 90% of the root causes come from the system not the individual. There is a strong tendency to assume that every problem is special. It is futile exhorting people to try harder without empowering and supporting them to work on the system itself. This is as true throughout communities as it is within manufacturing.

Two Mistakes

If people cannot distinguish between special and common causes they are likely to take actions which could do more harm than good. There are two mistakes that can be made (36). Mistake one is to react to an outcome as if it came from a special cause, when it actually came from common causes of variation. Mistake two, the opposite, is to react to an outcome as if it came from common causes of variation, when it actually came from a special cause.

Self-employment is a rapidly growing area of employment throughout the West. Self-employed people often have to live with large amounts of variation in their monthly income. There can be a tendency to treat every variation as if it were special. People make statements like this was a 'good month' or a 'bad one'. It is very possible that this variation is common cause and that the system is perfectly stable. If the data are plotted on a graph over time, often referred to as a Run Chart, it might become very apparent how stable the system is. There will be a mean monthly income and a degree of variation around the mean. The variation may be very high but still not special. If the system remains the same then the same performance can be expected. If the person makes mistake number one and thinks that each single month is special they may decide to take special action. If the self-employed person has had several 'bad' months, he or she may be tempted to do some extra promotion. If the system is stable it is very likely that the third month will be better, regardless of any action. If, as a result of the promotion, the person has generated many new leads they might find that, with the 'pick up' in business, they are unable to make initial meetings. This may have the effect of reducing their credibility in the market place, which could actually do harm to their existing business. These variations in income are not special. Treating them as such could lead to tampering. In this case it would be better to have done nothing. If the person really wanted to improve income they would have to work on the system itself, reviewing ways of booking work, increasing available resources or reviewing pricing policy. These are common cause interventions, which might reduce common cause variation and in this case increase the mean permanently.

Mistake number one occurs throughout communities. Crime figures vary month by month. Of course they will. The question has to be 'what are they telling us?' In many situations the crime statistics are perfectly stable. 'Knee jerking' just because the level has attracted the attention of the media or some politician is unlikely to address the real root causes in the community wide system. In these cases communities will often turn to the latest programme or fad for a quick fix. It is unlikely to do any good and could in some cases do more harm. The causes for crime are systemic and can not be dealt with by short-term interventions.

The example to highlight mistake number two is somewhat unpleasant but there are some important lessons. In spring 1996 Britain was shaken to the core by possibly one of the worst tragedies to occur in recent times. Thomas Hamilton, a gun-obsessed loner, walked into Dunblane Primary School and murdered 16 infants and their teacher. The whole world was shocked. There have been incidents in which more people have died but never so many innocent young children being gunned down in an environment that everyone thought was safe. The first priority was to do everything to support the parents and the wider community. An enquiry was held to see what lessons could be learnt. People started to call for much greater security in schools, the tightening of gun licensing and the parents, particularly, for the banning of all handguns in private ownership. Some of these responses may be appropriate but for other reasons. There is no doubt that this was a special cause. The number of children murdered in UK schools has been zero, or almost zero, for years. The danger now is that because of the atrocity, society may over compensate. There are many schools now reviewing security procedures. Some are going down the path of 'fortifying'. If schools are made into 'prisons' children will start to behave as prisoners. We will have changed the system because of a special cause and it could have a long-term effect on the overall performance of all schools. Ironically, fortification is unlikely even to prevent another Dunblane.

As a corollary to this example it is important to state that general violence has been on the increase in UK schools. This comes from common causes such as the breakdown of families, under-investment in education and discriminatory, outdated education processes. Schools do need to look at ways of tackling these systemic problems but putting up metal detectors at school entrances has not worked in the US and will not in the UK. We have to learn to distinguish between root causes and symptoms. Tackling symptoms has never been the best long-term strategy.

A less controversial example of mistake number two occurs in learning environments, both in schools and other organisations. A trainer or teacher may find that one or two people are struggling. This is possibly a special cause and these individuals need special assistance. If the trainer or teacher is not careful they may be tempted to change the overall learning process and could reduce the quality of learning for all the other students. If there is a common cause problem then the solution lies in the system and not with individual students. They have to be enabled to work, with the teacher, on the system itself.

The media has a specific responsibility in reducing the risk of making the two mistakes. The media often takes special causes and communicates them in a way to convince the public that they are common causes. For example, a horrendous mugging takes place of an old person. This is blazoned on the front pages of the newspapers. Many old people now start to think that this is likely to happen and this undermines their way of life. Britain is statistically one of the safest Western nations in terms of crime. However, the fear of crime is now more of a problem than crime itself.

Leaders can also do a lot of harm. Politicians regularly intervene in the running of public services, making special causes appear common. The MP's letter is a great example. Someone has an experience, writes to an MP and that MP then takes up the issue with the relevant department. All normal work is postponed as everyone rushes to respond. The disturbance can be very great. Leaders within organisations can be just as skilled at doing this.

The safest way to try to avoid making either of the two mistakes (37) is use data wisely. Statistical Process Control techniques such as Run Charts and Control Charts (38) are beyond the scope of this book but they should be investigated. In the absence of numerical data, the principles of variation still apply even if a chart cannot be produced. Understanding variation is central to managing stakeholder partnerships.

Measurement Good Practice

A process may have many outputs. Each output may have many customers. Each customer may have many wants and needs. Each want and need could have many measures. It is very easy to get overwhelmed by measurement. It is necessary to prioritise ruthlessly. Twenty percent of the measures will probably provide 80% of the useful information. Do not be tempted to measure what is easy. Concentrate on what is important, particularly to the customers of the process. Once the priorities have been identified it can then be assessed whether they are in fact measurable. Remember that some of the most important information is unknown or unknowable. It may not be possible to use quantitative means. 'Softer', more qualitative, measures may be required in the absence of useful 'hard', numerical measures or even to complement them. Soft measures are based on perceptions, feelings and views and, like 'hard' measures, have to be used cautiously. If in doubt get the advice of an expert, particularly a statistician.

If manipulation and 'games playing' are to be avoided it is very important to create an atmosphere of trust. When stakeholders have high levels of ownership they are less likely to manipulate figures consciously or unconsciously. Ownership can only come through direct involvement. The stakeholders are the people who should be agreeing operational definitions, setting targets and monitoring progress. When targets are imposed there is often fear and resentment. If people's pay is dependent on the targets there is a temptation to negotiate the targets down to the minimum. When the people who do the work set targets, they are often more challenging and there is greater commitment to achieving them. When measurement is founded on trust and inclusiveness, teams often far exceed their wildest expectations.

All users of data must understand variation. If they do not understand the basic concepts of common and special causes of variation they could be doing more harm than good. This presents a challenge. Many stakeholders have had no formal training. Many find statistics overwhelming. People facilitating stakeholder groups must find simple and novel ways of conveying these most important concepts.

In all the details about collecting and using data it is easy to lose sight of why it is being done. Measures are used to drive improvement. Information is often expensive. If the benefit derived from using it is not substantially greater than the cost of producing it, do not produce it. Information that is produced and not used is a substantial cost of failure within organisations and communities. Data is more likely to be used if the stakeholders 'own' it.

Measures reflect the performance of processes. Processes are usually highly interdependent and so are measures. Improving one measure may have the effect of driving several others down. A naive overdependence on one measure could be very harmful. It may be necessary to have a series of measures which produce an overall result. In aluminium extrusion four or five measures were used to give an overall assessment of extrusion press performance. They included speed of extrusion, scrap rates and press utilisation. On one site the production manager only ever asked about tonnage extruded. As a consequence everyone in this system put excessive emphasis on tonnage at the expense of delivery performance and production efficiency. Another example was of a purchasing manager saving money by buying flipchart paper without holes! The purchasing department reduced its expenditure by a few pounds but stores had to drill the holes manually. As a consequence labour costs were increased in the stores. However, this example only came to light when the flipchart paper would not fit on the easel. Now the downstream effect included wasting the time of a trainer and 20 delegates. This is an extreme example of sub-optimising but it is more common than one might imagine. Be wary of downstream effects and don't become over dependent on any one measure.

If groups of stakeholders, working to improve processes, take into account all of the warnings about measurement and systematically apply best practice, the measures will serve them well. They will help them understand the process, enable them to develop theories and provide evidence of successful improvement. It is not measures that are at fault; it is the poor way in which we use them. Effective measurement will never be achieved in a low trust, fearful environment.

Interdependence

Understanding systems inevitably leads to the subject of interdependence. Even a simple flowchart shows very clearly how internal customers and suppliers are dependent on one another to achieve the overall aims of the system. Communities are completely interdependent. Business, government, education and the voluntary sector depend on each other to function effectively. There are some basic principles of interdependence which are highly relevant to stakeholding.

Win/Win

This term has now entered common parlance but there are many subtleties contained within this somewhat trite expression. The first is to recognise that stakeholders have self-interests. It is futile and ultimately destructive to try and ignore these. In John Carlisle's book *Beyond Negotiation* he states the following. 'It is particularly clear in business dealings between firms that self-interest is a prime motive for doing most things. None of us today will live long enough to change that, even if we felt it helpful to do so. It is far more useful to accept self-interest as an initial force shaping the actions on both sides of any important relationship and to proceed to find ways to work with it' (39). This conclusion, derived from many years' experience working in the private sector, is equally applicable to all stakeholder relationships. They need to be founded on understanding each other's wants and needs. Caution is needed because these requirements may not be clearly stated at the start of a relationship. They may have to be 'teased out' over a period of time.

Once stakeholders' wants and needs are understood win/win relationships can be explored. There are several potential outcomes in a relationship between two stakeholders. These are win/lose, lose/win, lose/lose and, of course, win/win. Steven Covey has added a most important further possible outcome: no deal. Anything other than win/win or no deal will ultimately, in the long term, end up at lose/lose. Someone who feels that they have been taken advantage of in a particular relationship is unlikely to return unless for some reason they have no choice. It is common to try to involve communities in regeneration projects. Much of this is based on consultation rather than facilitation but the effect can often be to raise expectations unrealistically. As a consequence people in the community often feel let down and are unlikely to take part in future consultations. This will lead to the agencies being ineffective and so both parties have lost.

'No deal' requires great courage and is usually only feasible at the start of a potential relationship. If either party seriously doubts that a win/win is a likely outcome then they have to conclude that it is better not to enter into the relationship. Salespeople face this dilemma daily. Usually, due to the nature of sales reward systems, they will tend to go for the immediate gains. Several years ago a salesperson working for a well-respected computer company decided to turn down a very lucrative deal. The potential customer, a local authority, was convinced that this was the best solution for them. The salesperson was not. He was under intense pressure to close the deal but he had the courage of his convictions and turned down the opportunity to sell, providing very clear explanations why. As a result the trust he had created with the organisation increased. He found himself being invited to strategic planning sessions and getting open access to all the key players, every salesperson's dream. Eventually the local authority did purchase a system from him but it was much more appropriate to their real needs. The initial 'no deal' led ultimately to a long-term win/win.

The theory of win/win is central to stakeholding but the practice is problematic. The ideal is that all stakeholders benefit. However, this is not always achievable. The more stakeholders there are the greater the likelihood that someone is going to be disappointed. It may well be necessary for one stakeholder group to take a loss for the majority to gain which requires careful management. If one group consistently losses they are likely to withdraw from the partnership. Expectations need to be managed carefully, but this is not possible unless stakeholders' wants and needs are recognised and respected.

Commitment Levels

Relationships are very dynamic. Certain actions will increase the strength of the relationship. Other actions will undermine it. Each stakeholder will be on a continuum varying from low commitment to very high commitment. They will enter into the relationship at a particular level. It is important to appreciate where they are and in which direction their commitment is moving. Covey refers to this as the Emotional Bank Account (40). Actions that build trust are 'deposits'. Actions that reduce trust are 'withdrawals'. If one party makes too many withdrawals relative to deposits the other party might decide to 'close the account'. This happens quite often in stakeholder relationships. Take the real example of a world-famous manufacturer that announced in its strategic summary that it was committed to investing in its staff. It publicly committed to the UK national standard called Investors in People. Several months later it announced that it was making all of its latest apprentices redundant before they took up post-training roles. It also announced that staff would be subjected to a pay freeze. In the meantime the directors awarded themselves 40-50% bonuses. Within hours of this final announcement most of the staff had 'closed the account' on the leadership. Their Total Quality programme suffered particularly badly. Why should staff be bothered to make improvements if there is nothing in it for them?

Covey has identified six major ways of building trust in personal relationships that, with minor reinterpretation can be applied to stakeholding in communities. The six 'deposits' are:

- Really understand the stakeholders. This includes their wants as well as their needs and their world. This can be done in many ways including spending time with stakeholders in their environment.

- Attend to the 'little things'. Treating people with courtesy, respect and thanking them pays great dividends. These things cost little but can make the difference between success and failure.

- Keep commitments. Breaking promises is a sure way of undermining partnership working. If a key stakeholder makes a promise they must do everything in their means to deliver. If you doubt that you can do it, don't promise it.

- Clarify expectations. Based on understanding each other's wants and needs, stakeholders can start to manage each other's expectations. Unrealistic expectations usually lead to disappointment and undermine relationships.

- Show personal integrity. Integrity embraces everything else in this list. As Confucianism highlights 'A good man is ashamed to let his words outrun his deeds'.

- If withdrawals are made recognise this and try to reduce the impact. Apologies may be appropriate but empathy and consideration are essential too.

Win/win thinking is an aspiration. It is not always practical but it is a useful way of thinking. It is ultimately about understanding others' wants and needs as well as your own and should be a starting point in establishing stakeholder partnerships.

Scarcity and Abundance Thinking

There are those people who tend to think in scarcity terms. They believe that if they are going to do better, others will have to do worse. The usual metaphor is that of the pie. Scarcity people think in terms of a fixed size pie. These people tend to be very competitive and often negotiate win/lose relationships. Abundance thinkers, on the other hand, believe that by collaborating they can make the pie bigger and everyone can do better. They tend to be natural win/win thinkers and better at managing complex partnerships.

Unfortunately reality can get in the way of these concepts. Some situations are designed around scarcity thinking. A particular case is government funding. Often funds are fixed and stakeholders are encouraged to compete for them. Even if a partnership approach is encouraged, there often comes a point when funds have to be divided up. This can be a 'make or break point' and weak partnerships often disintegrate as everyone races to get their 'snouts' in the 'funding trough'. The Australian ambassador gave an interesting global example of abundance thinking to the US in a recent address in Honolulu. He had explained Australia's strategy of developing closer links with their East Asian neighbours. His experience was that others, such as the US, felt this might weaken existing relationships but as he explained this is not a 'zero sum situation'. Having stronger links with emerging economies does not necessarily prevent existing relationships strengthening too.

Maturity

Organisations, like individuals, go through stages as they mature. Covey has defined three levels of personal maturity: dependence, independence and interdependence (41). Children are very dependent on their parents but as they grow older they should be allowed to develop a sense of independence. Some unfortunate adults never manage to mature and they remain dependent on a spouse or relative. Independence is not the highest state of being in this model. Interdependence can only be arrived at after the other stages have been passed through. The simplest way to explain this is that an interdependent person knows that they are okay and that others are okay and that in order to be really effective they need to work closely with others. Interdependence is about achieving synergy. This model has commonalties with Transactional Analysis (42). People who understand themselves and their ancestry well have the freedom to chose appropriate ego states in which to operate. In organisations this is likely to be adult to adult most of the time. This minimises the risk of bringing personal dysfunction into stakeholder relationships.

Several years ago in a seminar on this subject a delegate pointed out that maybe nations have to go through similar stages too. By the Seventies Britain had become a highly dependent society. Many people believed that it was central government's responsibility to solve their problems. Thatcherism put a rapid end to collectivism and introduced rampant individualism. Self-interest was good. No one was going to look after you. There was no such thing as society. The Nineties reflect a very different view. People are feeling that there have to be better ways. Communities have been undermined and whilst an individual might be doing very well they do have collective responsibilities. Maybe Britain is moving out of independence into interdependence based on stakeholding. Hopefully the country is not returning to dependence.

Peoples' and organisations' maturity will have an effect on how well they can participate in stakeholder partnerships. In some cases there may have to be some foundational work to help people accept win/win thinking, abundance thinking and to accept interdependence.

Part 2

Practice of Stakeholding

Chapter 4

Who are the Stakeholders?

Identifying Stakeholders

How do leaders of organisations, or leaders of partnerships of organisations, or community leaders identify and understand their stakeholders? The first stage is to define the boundaries of the process. This enables the customers, partners, controllers and those who are in the core to be identified. Processes can be viewed at any level. At the lower levels the process may be embedded in an organisation or even in a function within an organisation. At higher levels the whole organisation can be considered as a process. The highest levels comprise viewing processes that embrace many interdependent organisations or even whole communities. It is very important to know the boundaries because this shows who operates within it and how it is outside. If one takes the approach too far, one ends up with everyone being stakeholders of every process. There are sensible 'cut off' points and the following examples should provide clarification.

Intra-organisational Processes

Process –   *Team briefing*

Purpose –   To ensure effective and rapid two-way communication up and
                   down the organisation.

Customers –   Staff being briefed (primary).
                   Management receiving feedback and questions (primary).
                   Actual customers receiving improved service as a consequence
                   of team briefing (secondary).

Core –	Team briefers who conduct the briefing.
	Senior management team who set the agendas to carry out the briefing process.
Partners –	Consultants who helped the organisation design and implement team briefing.
Controllers –	Industry bodies who might be able to give guidance on team briefing best practice.
	Other bodies that might have mandated team briefing.

Process –	*Maintain vehicle fleet*
Purpose –	To ensure that all vehicles are in a safe, roadworthy condition available as and when required.
Customers –	Drivers using the vehicles (primary).
	Schedulers, planning the use of the vehicles (primary).
	Actual customers requiring products distributed (secondary).
Core –	Garage manager.
	Fitters.
Partners –	Suppliers of the vehicles, spares and maintenance information.
Controllers -	Ministry of Transport which sets safety standards and other legal requirements.
	Financial director who sets maintenance budget.

Organisations as Processes

Organisation –	*Secondary School*
Key purpose –	To develop confident and competent life-long learners prepared for the future.
Customers –	Students who have 'graduated' from the school (primary).
	Parents seeing their children meeting their full potential (primary).
	Employers, who recruit effective, motivated team players (secondary).
	Community welcoming people with a strong sense of citizenship (secondary).

Higher and Further Education receiving students with maturity to continue their learning (secondary).

Future families of the students having better opportunities because of their parents' education (secondary).

Core –   Students currently at the school.

Teachers.

Administrators.

Support staff.

Partners –   Parents.

Supply teachers.

Feeder schools.

Cluster schools.

Employers.

Controllers – Department for Education.

Local Education Authority.

Board of Governors.

Organisation - **Construction Company**

Key Purpose – Exceed customers expectations in the design, construction and maintenance of living and working environments.

Customers –   Organisations requiring living and working environments (primary).

Users of the building including staff and visitor especially those with special needs (secondary).

Local community and the environment wanting minimum disturbance and aesthetically pleasing environments (secondary).

Core –   Company architects, planners, surveyors and site managers.

Senior management.

Administrative and support staff.

Partners –   Consultants.

Staff of partnering firms.

Sub-contractors.

Controllers –   Health and Safety Executive.

Parent company.

Local government planners.

Community-wide Processes

Process –   *Provision of a new hospital*

Purpose –   To provide a first rate health care environment on time and within budget.

Customers –   New patients (primary).

Health care staff (primary).

Families of patients (secondary).

Core –   Health Trust.

Property Services Management Organisation.

Partners –   Design and build construction company.

Controllers –   National Health Service Executive.

Health & Safety Executive.

Private financiers under the Private Finance Initiative (PFI).

Process –   *Crime prevention initiative*

Purpose –   To reduce the impact of crime on the local community.

Customers –   Local residents including the elderly, young people, businesses, people from ethnic minorities, etc.

Core –   Co-ordinating Charity.

County Council.

Police Service.

Partners –   Other voluntary sector organisations.

Schools.

Businesses.

Community Action Groups.

Controllers –   Home Office guidelines and targets on crime prevention.

An assortment of funding bodies.

The above examples highlight how stakeholders can be identified at any level as long as the process is clearly defined. Process concepts and the categories of stakeholder should help any leader identify his or her stakeholders. This has to be done, at least roughly, before plans can be made how to understand and engage stakeholders.

Chapter 5

How to Engage Stakeholders

Stakeholders can be engaged in many different ways throughout organisations and partnerships of organisations. They can be engaged at different stages in the design and delivery of service and to varying degrees. Before these options can be considered it is useful to examine models of organisations and partnerships.

Best Practice

In recent years much effort has been expended trying to define what is best practice in organisations. It has become fashionable to 'benchmark' against those that are supposed to the best in the world. In order to do this an operational definition of 'best' is required. Many national and international consultancy companies and professional bodies have risen to the challenge and produced their own models. Few have been widely adopted and each has been different in its emphasis and structure. In the last ten years two models have been developed which have gained worldwide acceptance: the Malcolm Baldrige National Quality Award in the US and the Business Excellence Model in Europe (43).

Quality Awards

The origins of these models go back to the early Fifties in Japan. The Japanese Union of Scientists and Engineers (JUSE) were looking for a means of promoting Total Quality Control at a national level. It was considered that a very prestigious award would help inspire others on their quality journeys. JUSE launched the Deming Prize, named in recognition of one of the Americans that had inspired them. The Deming

Prize is not very transparent but it is keenly contested and has certainly motivated many of Japan's largest corporations. It has very high exposure each year, so much so that several US firms have competed.

As quality became fashionable in the West pressure mounted in the US and Europe to follow suit with national and international awards. The US Malcolm Baldrige National Quality Award was second to market in 1988. This has proven remarkably successful not just in the award but particularly in the number of all types of organisations that have adopted the model for assessing themselves. Each year hundreds of organisations apply to win the awards but thousands of assessment information packs are distributed through both the public and private sectors.

In the late Eighties the European Foundation for Quality Management (EFQM) was formed by some of Europe's leading organisations. They too set about developing an award framework, which would become a definition for best practice. In 1992 the European Quality Award was launched. Very rapidly most of Europe's quality bodies set up national awards based on the same framework. In the UK the British Quality Foundation promotes the UK Quality Award. There are now many regional versions and businesses, hospitals, the police and even schools, are using the framework. In 1995 the underpinning framework was renamed the Business Excellence Model in recognition of the breadth of the model.

Best Practice in Organisations

The simple premise behind the Business Excellence Model (BEM) is that excellent organisations achieve excellence in both what they do and what they achieve. The model divides equally between enablers – what you do – and results, what you achieve. There are many different ways of assessing how well an organisation is doing compared to this standard of excellence (44). In fact the real value of this approach is not as an award, with a very limited number of winners, but as a framework for assessment.

The more detailed premise is that business results, or more general organisational success, will only be achieved when 'delighted customers boast about the service and bring their friends with them' (45). This level of customer satisfaction will be achieved when staff is highly satisfied and motivated. Another influence on business results and both customer and people satisfaction is the way in which the community perceives the organisation. An excellent organisation invests in its local community. These four criteria, business results, customer satisfaction, people satisfaction and impact on society, are all results. They will only be achieved if the organisation adopts certain methods or ways of working.

The means to achieving the results are the organisation's processes. These deliver the range of products and services to the customers. They need to be underpinned with very clear strategy and policy. If processes are to function well they need the right resources in terms of money, information, raw materials and equipment as well as people. People need to be recruited, inducted and trained well. Communication needs to be the best it possibly can be. Finally the cornerstone of all excellence is the quality of leadership. Leaders need to 'walk the talk' and lead from the front. Everyone contributes to excellence but leaders have the responsibility for facilitating the removal of the barriers that prevent the rest of the stakeholders getting on with the job.

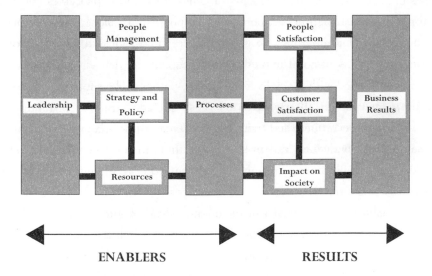

Figure 11. The EFQM's Nine-Block Business Excellence Model

A nine-block model is used to summarise the Business Excellence Model (Figure 11). In summary, customer satisfaction, people satisfaction and positive impact on society are achieved through leadership driving policy and strategy, people management, resources and processes, leading ultimately to excellence in results.

The BEM presents the key elements of a successful organisation in a very clear, succinct way. Stakeholders can be engaged in all of the criteria, although it may not be appropriate to have all people represented all of the time.

It is important to engage stakeholders in defining and agreeing measures. They should be closely involved in setting and monitoring the results criteria. In a limited company shareholders should wish to be closely involved in agreeing the measures for business results. These should be more than just financial measures. Shareholders should take a keen interest in the rest of the model, but few do. Obviously customers, and staff close to customers, should be engaged in setting up the critical measures for customer satisfaction. The staff should be the key stakeholders to deciding how to monitor people satisfaction.

Another way to look at the enablers is to subdivide them into delivery processes and support processes. Delivery processes include all the activities that generate the products or services. In a manufacturing organisation delivery processes cover design right through to distribution and post sales support. In a school, delivery processes embrace all the learning processes from curriculum development through to assessment, including pastoral processes. In a hospital the delivery processes include everything concerned with the delivery of care to patients. The support processes tend to be more generic to all organisations. They include strategic planning, people processes such as recruitment and training, and development and resource deployment processes such as budgeting and procurement. It is more problematic to consider leadership in purely process terms. There are process elements but there are psychological issues too.

So the enablers in the BEM can be broadly divided into delivery and support processes. If any of these processes are to be improved then the specific stakeholders need to be represented. For example, if an organisation is reviewing its style of leadership then obviously leaders need to be engaged but so do the staff and certain controllers. It may even be useful to involve some key customers. If a delivery process is being reviewed then primary and possibly secondary customers will need to be included. If recruitment is being investigated the stakeholders will include those recruiting and those recently recruited.

The Business Excellence Model is rapidly becoming accepted as a 'standard' of best practice within all types of organisations. Using stakeholding principles will ensure that organisations get better results from the model. Stakeholders can be engaged in establishing and monitoring the results criteria as well as being actively involved in improving all delivery and support processes.

Best Practice in Partnerships of Organisations

Partnership is now a politically correct word. Most organisations make reference to it in their vision and mission statements. Because of the entrenched reductionism and compartmentalisation in Western communities, implementing partnerships is proving to be much more difficult. Governments call on sectors to work in closer partnerships and then go and create systemic barriers to this way of working, particularly in funding and monitoring. Organisations have to form working partnerships far more rapidly than ever before. People from different organisational cultures, often with very different agendas, have to work more closely. However the Business Excellence Model is a useful model for partnerships too.

Partnerships, even more so than single organisations, need to:

- be clear about whom they exist to serve.
- establish useful, robust ways of measuring performance.
- ensure that processes are defined, assured and continually improved.
- have clear, shared, responsive strategies.
- train and develop staff from the different organisations rapidly to create a common business culture.
- communicate rapidly and effectively.
- allocate resources equitably and transparently.
- ensure cohesive, principle-centred leadership.

With care the BEM can be adapted to cover even the most complex of partnerships and can be used to ensure that the partnership achieves best practice as well as the constituent organisations.

Principles of Best Practice

The Business Excellence Model embraces very broad methods for achieving certain results. All methods are based on underpinning values and principles. There is no such thing as value-free human behaviour. Unfortunately some organisations have embraced the BEM but without embracing the deeper principles. They will not succeed in the long run.

Consultants and academics have debated the underlying principles of management for centuries. Accepted wisdom has evolved and is a function of current social and political beliefs. Some experts surmise that certain principles are fundamental, unarguable laws of nature or even 'God given' (46). Whether principles are relative or absolute is not the subject of this book. What is in contention is that underlying values and principles, whether expressed explicitly or not, have a large impact on the success of methods such as stakeholding and excellence.

It is important for all organisations and partnerships, no matter how temporary, to consider their shared values and principles. There are few, clearly articulated, summaries of such principles that have real depth. A much more profound understanding is required than the 'happy clappy' approach offered by many of the popularist management 'gurus'. Dr Deming, over a long lifetime of service, developed such a list, the 14 points, and the system of profound knowledge. Whilst no concept is 'perfect', Deming's work is an excellent starting point.

The system of profound knowledge provides a lens or a new map of theory by which to understand organisations (47). It is certainly a major paradigm shift. According to Deming profound knowledge comprises four parts:

- Appreciation for a system.
- Knowledge about variation.
- Theory of knowledge.
- Understanding of psychology.

Chapter 3 has already covered much about systems and variation and material on learning and psychology is spread throughout the book. The 14 points follow naturally from profound knowledge. The 14 points are not a prescription. In fact the name is a misnomer. It would be better to refer to them as principles or even obligations to leadership. They are summarised here. Each point could require a lifetime's study to truly master and for readers who wish to know more it is recommended to study the texts in the references.

Dr Deming's 14 Points:

1. Create constancy of purpose toward improvement of products and services, with the aim to become competitive, to stay in business and to provide jobs.

2. Adopt a new philosophy. We are in a new economic age. Western management must awaken to the challenges, must learn their responsibilities and take on leadership for change.

3. Cease dependence on inspection to achieve quality. Eliminate the need for inspection on a mass basis by building quality into the product or service in the first place.

4. End the practice of awarding business on the basis of price tag. Instead, minimise total cost. Move toward a single supplier for any one item, on a long-term relationship of loyalty and trust.

5. Improve constantly and forever the system of production and service, to improve quality and productivity and thus constantly decrease costs.

6. Institute training on the job.

7. Institute leadership. The aim of leadership should be to help people and machines and gadgets to do a better job. Leadership of management is in need of overhaul, as well as leadership of production workers.

8. Drive out fear, so that everyone may work effectively for the company.

9. Break down the barriers between departments. People in research, design, sales and production must work as team, to foresee problems of production and in use that may be encountered.

10. Eliminate slogans, exhortations and targets for the workforce asking for zero defects and new levels of productivity.

11. Eliminate work standards (quotas) on the factory floor. Eliminate management by objective. Eliminate management by numbers, numerical goals. In their place substitute leadership.

12. Remove the barriers that rob the all staff of their right to pride in workmanship.

13. Institute a vigorous programme of education and self-improvement.

14. Put everyone to work to accomplish the transformation. The transformation is everybody's job.

Deming wrote the 14 points primarily for the manufacturing sector. They have subsequently been interpreted for all types of organisations including service companies and schools. They are universal. The language is a little outdated but the spirit is sound.

It is possible to adopt the Business Excellence Model founded on the 14 points and profound knowledge. If organisations do not do so they will not get the full benefits and could cause more harm. Table 1 shows the linkages between the 14 points and the criterion of the BEM.

The Business Excellence Model, based on the 14 points and profound knowledge, provides a powerful framework for engaging stakeholders in organisations and partnerships of organisations.

Criteria of BEM Dr Deming's 14 Points/Principles	Leadership	Policy and Strategy	People Management	Resources	Process	People Satisfaction	Customer Satisfaction	Impact on Society	Business Results
1 Create constancy of purpose	Medium	Strong				Strong	Strong	Strong	Strong
2 Adopt the new philosophy	Strong								
3 Cease dependence on inspection					Medium				
4 Minimise total cost				Medium	Medium				
5 Improve all processes constantly					Strong				
6 Institute training on the job			Strong						
7 Institute leadership	Strong	Medium							
8 Drive out fear			Weak			Weak			
9 Break down barriers between depts.					Strong				
10 Eliminate exhortation and slogans			Weak						
11 Eliminate quotas and goals		Weak	Weak		Weak				
12 Remove the barriers to pride in work			Medium			Medium			
13 Institute education and self-improvement			Weak						
14 Put everyone to work on transformation			Medium			Medium	Medium		

Table 1. Table showing the relationship between the BEM and the 14 Points

Legend: Degree to which Criterion embraces Principles — Strong   Medium   Weak   <blank> —not at all

Stages of Stakeholder Engagement

The development of all products, services, organisations and partnerships go through discrete stages or 'life cycles'. They are planned, delivered, reviewed and improved. Eventually they may be decommissioned. Stakeholders can be engaged at the various stages in a variety of different ways.

Planning

This involves engaging stakeholders at a strategic level, at the start of the design of processes. The types of activities include: understanding who is being served, clarification of need, visioning and setting strategic priorities. Early involvement of stakeholders can save embarrassment, time and money. It is possible that in understanding customers' wants and needs it might become apparent that the process is not required or should be very different to the original concept. Communication will improve, particularly concerning related work that might have gone on in the past or is ongoing. Stakeholder groups will have the opportunities to understand each other's constraints, which will build empathy and should reduce conflict. Ultimately there should be greater consensus and ownership as a result of strategic involvement.

More detailed planning will be required to convert the overall strategy into practical implementation plans. Problems may arise with fund allocation and deadlines that may be specific to a stakeholder group. The more involvement, the more likely that these differences can be resolved quickly and amicably. Involvement in detailed planning is likely to increase the commitment of different groups to achieve the plans. Most people do not mind change. It is *being* changed that they resent.

Delivery

This is the acid test. If the planning stage has been effective then delivery should be relatively straightforward. Now is the real test of the commitment of the stakeholder groups. It is essential to ensure that groups are capable of delivering. This is often referred to as capacity building. Some stakeholder groups have been systematically disempowered for hundreds of years. To expect these people to take an immediate role in delivery is unrealistic. Confidence levels may have to be built by sensitive and effective training. Formal training may be alienating so other means such as coaching, on-the-job learning or self-teach methods may have to be considered. Some groups may need a lot of support and encouragement. Regular feedback is important.

Reviews

It is very important to establish mechanisms for review and evaluation at the design stage. Too many teams get to the end of a project and have difficulty in assessing success because this was never precisely defined in the first place. Effective evaluation starts at design and should be conducted regularly throughout the life of the project. Regular reviews with stakeholders should enable corrective actions to be taken rapidly and with little expenditure. People must feel safe to state things as they see them. There is little point ignoring this feedback but leaders do need to be able to discern genuine problems from anxiety or self-interest. Reviews also highlight the need to review direction and strategy. Plans should never be so inflexible that they cannot be changed if circumstances have changed. Keeping close to stakeholders will minimise the risk of be intransigence.

Improvements

Regular reviews should identify strategic and tactical improvements. Involving stakeholders will often lead to a greater range of improvement ideas. Some of these may be impractical but if people are open there could be one or two very innovative and practical new ways of doing things. The people nearest to the process are likely to be best able to assess what is feasible. Improvements, once generated need to be planned, implemented and reviewed themselves. Different stakeholders may need to be involved at the improvement stage depending on the specifics of the situation.

Engaging stakeholders in strategic planning and process improvement is so important it forms the basis of the next two chapters.

Styles of Engagement

Leaders have a range of options in the ways in which they engage stakeholders. They are based on very different styles. Each may be appropriate at certain times depending on the specific requirements. There are at least four distinct options: tell, sell, consult and facilitate (Figure 12).

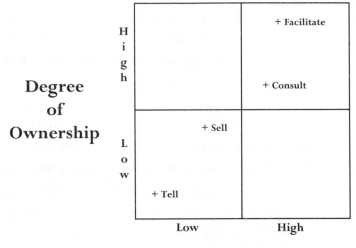

Figure 12. Grid showing different leadership styles

The 'tell' option is straightforward. A group of stakeholders, usually the leaders, make a decision and tell other groups. This can be done rapidly but is unlikely to create much ownership. Some people feel secure in this paternalistic situation because it absolves them of responsibility. If anything goes wrong it is easy to blame others. Don't always assume that stakeholder groups are ready or even keen to be empowered.

The 'sell' approach is slightly more time consuming and is based on one stakeholder group convincing others of the benefits of their solution. There are degrees of selling depending on the power relationships between stakeholders. A leader selling an idea to his or her subordinates may not experience much resistance, but if there is little positional power selling may be more difficult.

Consultation is often thinly disguised telling. In true consultation people are presented with a range of options and the comments received are taken into account in the final decision. The final decision usually rests with the body initiating the consultation. Ownership can be greater in consultation but it can become tokenistic, especially if good feedback is not given.

Facilitation is a very different style. It is about guiding a group of stakeholders though a process in order to reach a group decision. A professional facilitator does not influence the actual outcome but guides the process by which the outcome is achieved. It shares many common traits with counselling. There is merit in the facilitator not be ing too familiar with the issue or process. Facilitators must be impartial so it is often important to select a credible outsider. There must be no hidden agendas and the facilitator must never do a 'Blue Peter', presenting a solution that he or she prepared earlier. Facilitation creates very high levels of ownership and commitment, if done properly, and hence leads to greater long-term effectiveness. Unfortunately it can take a considerable amount of time. However, when one considers the amount of time often wasted in projects by not getting consensus and understanding at the start, it can still be a cost-effective approach. Patience and tenacity will be required to use a facilitative style.

The challenge for leaders is to choose the appropriate style (48). Taking the wrong approach can undermine stakeholder partnerships. For example, bringing staff together to facilitate choosing the colour of the new tea towels would be wasteful and insulting. However, strategic planning is so important that not facilitating stakeholders would lead to many missed opportunities. Many leaders tell when they should facilitate and facilitate when they should tell. The different styles can be used at the different stages. For example, stakeholders could be told a plan or they could be facilitated. Improvements could be sold or stakeholders could be consulted over the options. Consider styles carefully and then choose the appropriate methods and tools. The next two chapters present methods and tools for engaging stakeholders in strategic planning and process improvement.

Chapter 6

Engaging Stakeholders in Strategic Planning

- What is the point of running fast in the wrong direction?

- Most 'improvement' is like rearranging the deckchairs on the *Titanic*!

- Empowerment without constancy and consistency of purpose is anarchy!

It is no accident that 'achieving constancy of purpose' was the first of Dr Deming's 14 Points. Without a clear sense of long-term direction an organisation or partnership is rudderless. Much energy in organisations is expended on doing rather than thinking. However, how can organisations assess whether they have arrived if they never clearly defined where they were going in the first place? Planning activities are as much 'real work' as any other activities and must be taken seriously.

Strategic planning is the highest level planning and hence should influence all subsequent activities. Strategic plans become idle fantasy unless there are processes to convert these ideals into tactical plans and actions. These plans, once implemented, need to be continually reviewed and improvement actions taken accordingly. This represents the most important application of the classic Shewart Cycle (49): plan, do, study and act. In this way strategic planning is a process that drives many other processes within the organisation. Problems arising in the strategic planning process will cascade and magnify throughout the rest of the organisation. Many of the root causes of problems in organisations have their origins in the boardroom.

There are some clear requirements for an effective strategic planning process. The process should:

- be rapid and flexible.
- be driven by customers.
- involve all stakeholders.
- anticipate and innovate.
- be continually improved.
- establish clear priorities.
- align and integrate all activities.

The days of one or two leaders retreating into expensive hotels to produce five-year plans for the organisation are over. For a start, plans can no longer afford to be inflexible and rigid. The rates of change in all areas of global life are so great that new opportunities and threats may emerge in days rather than years. The only way to cope is to have a flexible, responsive and sometimes informal, planning process that can be run frequently and quickly. Organisations need to be able to adjust direction more like speedboats than oil tankers. However, they do need to be careful that they don't change direction so frequently that they lose constancy and consistency of purpose and become like 'boats tossed around by the waves'.

Another reason why traditional methods of strategic planning are being challenged is the need to have all stakeholders understanding the direction and the priorities of the organisation and their personal contributions to the whole. The purpose of strategic planning is not to produce a document but to ensure that a similar vision is in everyone's 'hearts and minds'. Writing documentation is a relatively quick and easy process compared with achieving true constancy of purpose. Achieving shared vision takes years of hard work.

If strategic planning is a process then it can be improved like any other process. There is no such thing as a perfect strategy. How would an organisation know? Organisations can, however, work to improve the process continuously. Staff surveys can be used to highlight the levels of understanding and ownership of the plan.

Benchmarking will help identify best practice in strategic planning and Customer and Partner Workshops will identify the commitment of other stakeholders. This information can be used to identify issues or problems with the process, the root causes can be identified and improvements implemented.

This chapter is written around a process of strategic planning that has been applied in just about every type of organisation and partnership over the last ten years. It has been subject to continual improvement and utilises tools and techniques that are designed to engage large numbers of stakeholders. The process is cyclical and goes through several discrete stages:

- focusing on customers.
- anticipating influences.
- ensuring constancy of purpose.
- identifying critical success factors.
- prioritising and aligning processes.

Each stage is now considered in detail. Readers are encouraged to compare their own strategic planning processes to that presented here and to borrow and hone ideas if appropriate. Some of the more useful tools and techniques for strategic planning are included in Chapter 8.

Focusing on Customers

In the private sector it is easy to forget that markets comprise people, and people are often not as logical and reasonable as they like to think they are. In the public sector it is even easier to lose sight of the people actually being served and to focus all attention on the political 'masters'. In Chapter 2 stakeholders are classified into four categories: customers, controllers, partners and the core.

Customers are those people who receive the product or service. Primary customers receive it directly. They are the people for whom the original product or service was designed. Secondary customers receive the service indirectly, 'downstream' of the primary customers. Secondary customers include the customers of primary customers, the broader community and interest groups representing the environment. The term customer does not necessarily imply any financial transaction.

Controllers define, regulate and influence the organisation or process. Controllers include regulators, legislators, providers of capital including funders of voluntary and government services, the media and trustees. In some contexts, particularly in the public sector, where controllers directly fund services they have to be considered alongside primary and secondary customers.

Wants and Needs

Part of the aim of any process is continually to improve the service to the customers. However, the customer is not always right and serving customers is a complex balance of meeting their wants and their needs. If a person wants something they have generally recognised the requirement themselves. They may not perceive that they have other requirements or needs. So a customer may know that they want certain things but they may be less aware, or even ignorant, of some of their deeper and longer-term needs. In this context the customer defines the wants and the supplier the needs, and quality is about meeting and exceeding both wants and needs. It is the duty of the supplier to ensure that, through effective communication, both wants and needs are understood and agreed at the start of the process.

Organisations find themselves on a wants and needs continuum depending on the nature of the product or service that they provide. At one end of the spectrum are organisations such as fast food chains. Quality is defined as giving the customer what they want. 'You want it, you got it.' This approach would be highly inappropriate for organisations at the other end of the continuum such as medical practices and law firms. Due to the complexity of their services and the professional nature of the work, quality is much more than giving the customer what they say they want. These suppliers have to ensure that needs are met too. Most organisations have to satisfy a range of wants and needs. An organisation that moves too far to either extreme may experience difficulties. Even the fast food store has to consider the customers' less recognised needs such as nutrition and safety.

For many years local authorities worked on the basis that they knew best what people needed. Some became very patronising and isolated from their customer communities. Two neighbouring local authorities in the South West of England had very different strap lines. One was 'providing the services you need' and the second was 'serving you'. These rather trite statements reflected very different cultures and styles. One authority was focusing on engaging the community, the other was remote, centralist and generally unpopular. One of them no longer exists!

Organisations have to understand their customers' immediate and long-term wants and needs. Asking customers will not always reveal this information. The best way to get this understanding is to recognise the importance of customers and to keep so close to them that you anticipate their requirements before they do. Then the organisation can concentrate on meeting and hopefully exceeding these requirements.

Customer Behaviour

It is a mistake to think that individual customers behave in very logical and predictable ways. When customer behaviour is analysed collectively some patterns emerge that can have profound effects on the success of organisations. In the Eighties the US market research company TARP published findings which have been quoted ever since. They investigated the ways in which customers behave when receiving a range of commercial services where there is a wide range of suppliers and the costs of changing supplier are not great. Their findings are summarised below.

Out of 100 recipients of poor service typically only four will formally complain to the supplier. On average every person goes on to tell another ten people how bad their experience was. Therefore for every complaint received there could be as many as 250 people who have knowledge of the poor service. If the media is involved the effect of the 'complaints mushroom' is increased dramatically. A UK house builder recently built a handful of executive houses with a lethal mortar mix comprising mainly sand. The mortar could be scraped out from between the bricks and outside walls could be pushed over by hand! This company, probably on the advice of its accountants, decided that it could not afford repairs and contested the complaints from the homeowners. Eventually Members of Parliament and national television became involved. The real damage to this company was unmeasurable but it was one of the first to withdraw from house building during the most recent recession. The total cost was certainly more than replacing the houses with extra features as way of compensation. This example really highlights the dangers of working with visible figures alone. It is very difficult to predict the precise damage to an organisation in lost business due to the 'complaints mushroom' but this does not make the economic effect any the less real. Fortunately if an organisation 'overkills' on the resolution of a complaint this can limit the damage and it will also be told to other potential customers. Typically, the 'compliments mushroom' is half the size of the complaints one. People tend to tell twice as many people of bad news as good news.

TARP also discovered that 63% of buyers questioned decided to go to alternative suppliers due to personal service issues, not technical ones. Reasons for finally giving up on a supplier included promises not being kept, unfriendly staff, difficulty in making contact, patronising or sexist staff.

By studying specific situations of customer dissatisfaction the researchers discovered that on average acquiring a new customer costs five times that of retaining an existing one. If it is possible to win back a lost customer this costs nine times more. So much money is invested in winning new customers through advertising campaigns, that looking after existing customers is often a low priority. First Direct, the UK's first telephone bank, grew by the equivalent of a traditional branch a month, by concentrating on looking after existing customers and depending on their recommendations. A very targeted promotion campaign supported this successful strategy. This bank is living proof of Dr Deming's statement about profits coming from 'delighted customers boasting about your service and bringing their friends with them'.

Organisations cannot wait for customers to tell them what is wrong. At the very least they need to have accessible and easy-to-use complaints processes. Much more than this, organisations have to be proactive and listen continuously to the voice of their customers. This information must drive strategic planning as well as permeating all other processes.

While this research was based in the private sector, many of the findings apply to the public and voluntary sectors. In a 'not for profit' situation increasing customer satisfaction may or may not bring a direct financial benefit. This depends on the funding mechanisms for the organisation. There will be an increase in the value to the customers, and other stakeholders, which may be difficult to quantify. For example, a school which makes significant improvements in learning will improve its reputation. As a result more and more parents will wish to send their children there. If the school's funding is calculated per child then its budget will increase as a result of the improvements. This assumes spare capacity within the school. If the funds are calculated by a different formula there may be no immediate financial benefit to the school even though the real benefit to society could be substantial.

Customer Satisfaction

Customer satisfaction can be monitored on a scale from complete dissatisfaction to delight. Satisfaction is the difference between perception and expectation. The greater the expectation the harder it is to ensure that the perceived quality is greater. Customers will experience a certain level of satisfaction for a given set of circumstances. This will be influenced by three factors: those which cause dissatisfaction, satisfaction and delight.

Factors causing dissatisfaction may be undesirable processes or product features. When they are present, customer satisfaction decreases significantly. If no such factors are present, customer satisfaction is not improved; it simply does not deteriorate. These factors are considered much more significant by the customer than the organisation may realise. Examples include defective products or services, delivery problems, problems in obtaining service, uncooperative staff, or indifference to complaints or customer questions.

Factors causing satisfaction are expected processes or product features. As more of these factors are provided customer satisfaction increases. If the price of a product is reduced, it is better value and the customer is more satisfied. The offer of a wider range of product styles, models, i.e. choices, are factors causing satisfaction.

Factors causing delight are processes or features which were neither expected nor specified and are positively viewed by the customer when experienced. Often 'delight factors' cost little or can even be free. They are very personal. The Royal Crescent Hotel in Bath puts a local weather forecast for the next day into every room every day. Alamo Car Rentals use automated means for completing customer surveys. They are incredibly rapid, fun to use and placed where customers have to wait for airport buses so it helps pass the time. Casualty Departments in hospitals have started to distribute fact sheets for common ailments. They are clear and simple to understand. They alleviate a lot of concerns patients have about asking 'stupid questions' and remembering information.

A customer is eventually going to arrive at an overall level of satisfaction. Sometimes judgements are made very rapidly and it can be difficult to get people to change their minds. In some cases customers have got preconceptions that they want reinforced. This is particularly true of some public services. Daniel Kahnemann has shown that human recollections of pain and pleasure do not necessarily correspond to the actual experience. He has identified 'the peak and end rule' (50). The peak of emotion during an experience and how we felt when it ended conditions our memories. This is important for suppliers of products and services to understand. A 'happy ending' can mitigate against even very unpleasant experiences. Ultimately the assessment of overall satisfaction by the customer is a very personal process.

Factors causing dissatisfaction, satisfaction and delight interact. For example, trying to delight a dissatisfied customer might reduce or even negate the dissatisfaction. Sometimes it can exacerbate the situation. Several factors causing dissatisfaction will tend to have a cumulative effect greater than their individual effects. For example, if an airline manages to delay all of the flights on one journey this is far worse than the same number of delays over many journeys. If their approach to the problem is cavalier and they do little to support stranded passengers they are likely to have caused such great dissatisfaction that people will be determined never to use them again and also to convince their friends not to. Expectations tend only to ratchet upwards. What delights today will only satisfy tomorrow and if it goes wrong, it has the potential to dissatisfy.

Dimensions of Quality

Over many years of listening to customers common traits or dimensions of quality service start to emerge, even for very diverse products and services. Standard models for quality have been developed. One such model or framework is SERVQUAL (51).

SERVQUAL was developed by Parasuraman, Zeithaml and Berry. Through extensive research in different service sectors they concluded that it is possible to condense all service attributes into one of five categories. They are as follows:

Tangibles –   The appearance of physical facilities, equipment, personnel and communications materials.

Reliability –   The ability to perform the promised service dependably and with accuracy.

Responsiveness –   The willingness to help customers and to provide them with prompt service.

Assurance –   Knowledge and courtesy of employees and their ability to convey trust and confidence.

Empathy –   Caring, individualised attention that the organisation provides its customers.

'Off the shelf' models need to be used cautiously. The very process of engaging stakeholders in defining customers' wants and needs often leads to exciting opportunities. The rule is to assume nothing.

A mystery guest, along with a customer clinic and a stakeholder improvement workshop, led a hotel in Bath to produce a very comprehensive model of business customers' wants and needs. The five main dimensions were value for money, pre-stay experience, the stay itself, the post-stay experience and generic service issues. The generic service issues comprised staff knowledge and attitude and the complaints process. Pre-stay covered making the reservation and post-stay, the invoicing and follow up. The stay itself was broken down into arrival, environment and departure. Environment comprised the quality of both the personal and communal space. In total over one hundred wants and needs were identified and structured in this way. It even covered details such as getting access to the telephone socket in order to connect up a laptop fax/modem and not treating customers like idiots by giving them enormous and heavy key fobs!

The Voice of the Customer

There are many methods for obtaining and understanding the 'voice of the customer'. Marketing professionals have used some of them for many years. Others are newer and less conventional. The choice of method will depend on statistical validity, cost, time, closeness of relationship, the sophistication of your customers and other practical issues. The key is to be so close to your customers that you can anticipate their real short and long-term wants and needs.

It is not the purpose of this book to explore marketing techniques in detail. If a group of stakeholders wishes to carry out formal research they can use statistically valid approaches such as surveys and customer clinics. Surveys can be done face to face, through the mail or over the phone. Different approaches will get different response rates. Questionnaires can be used but they need to be designed very carefully and questions kept to the absolute minimum. The designers of the questionnaire will need to know the nature of the questions you wish to ask and the purpose. Do you use closed or open questions or both? How long will the questionnaire take? How will you get access to your customers? Are the questions culturally relevant? Do they favour one particular group? Remember some people have trouble with numeracy and literacy. The author heard of a case recently whereby a form sent by the Department for Social Security nearly led a person suffering from a mental illness to have a relapse! This was a fine example of customer care!

Customer clinics are useful when the volume and type of customer means that they are unlikely to participate directly in improvement or development activities. Do not waste people's valuable time. Treat them with respect and reward them in an appropriate way. Ensure that the clinics are well facilitated and use a variety of media to maintain interest.

Other, less conventional methods include engaging customers directly in the work to be done, being the customer and observing customers. Getting customers to participate actively in strategic planning and process improvement is invaluable, although it can be difficult. Consider the barriers that might exist, preventing full involvement. These can include language, fear of repercussions, disability, childcare provision and time of day. Do not be tempted to use these potential barriers as excuses. Most barriers can be removed. Students have been actively engaged in school development planning, unemployed people in the development of new services and people suffering serious mental illness in the improvement of day care services and even the design of new psychiatric hospitals. The results have been better services and less money wasted. Particularly in the public sector we need to move away from supply-driven services to customer-driven ones.

Powerful lessons can be learnt by being or observing customers. Senior managers, particularly, need to allocate time to spend with customers on a day-to-day basis. Care needs to be taken to adhere to the underpinning principles of quality. One chief executive of a Hospital Trust came into work in a wheelchair to discover what it was really like to be an outpatient. His intention was admirable but the results were used to blame rather than to drive process improvement. Another chief executive arrived at one of the airports that his organisation is responsible for managing with plenty of notice and received the 'red carpet' treatment. He was checked-in and on his way in less than three minutes. If only his customers got this kind of service!

Another method is to use 'mystery guests'. Again this can provide valuable information as long as it doesn't create fear and the results are not used to manipulate people. Work on improving the process. Don't blame people.

All of the above methods have merit. An organisation may use any combination of them. There are several things to be wary of. Firstly, what customers say and what they do can be very different. Sometimes people will tell you what they think that you want to hear rather than what you need to hear. Also customers are unlikely to be innovative. They tend to ask for more of the same. Innovation comes from being so close to customers that you anticipate their future wants and needs before they do. Finally, there needs to be some return for the customers. Some will gain directly through better quality service and less hassle. Others can be rewarded through the giving of appropriate gifts. Some may get involved for ulterior reasons. The organisation needs to be sure that it is not just listening to some special cases or special causes. Generally customers are the toughest stakeholders to get involved in meaningful and useful ways.

Customer Performance Indicators

In order to define the customers' true satisfaction level, the organisation should consider the various data collection methods. An organisation can identify customer satisfaction through quantitative or qualitative surveys. In quantitative surveys, data may be collected through interviews, questionnaires to be filled out by the customers, or through observation of customer behaviour. In qualitative surveys, the organisation may go into more detail on the surveyed questions, extract customer perceptions and become familiar with customer feelings. The organisation should define the best data collection methods in accordance with the nature of the study, deadlines and available funds.

Anticipating Influences

All the evidence suggests that those who spend concentrated time thinking about the future manage it better. They are unlikely to predict the future precisely but the process of reflection means that they respond more rapidly. A good example was the Shell Petroleum Company. In the early Seventies they implemented a comprehensive scenario planning process across all business divisions. They explored different global scenarios and how these could affect their business. No one predicted the Oil Crisis of the mid-Seventies but due to this reflective discipline Shell was able to respond more rapidly to the change than their competitors. It is a shame that by the Nineties they underestimated the importance of the environment to their customers.

By 1995 it was becoming increasingly apparent to people in the United Kingdom that a change of government was likely in 1997. Eighteen years of Conservative domination was coming to an end. Few predicted the scale of the Labour landslide and many were cautious because of the surprise return of the Tories in the previous election. In this climate of political turbulence the wise companies put aside their natural prejudices and started to build relationships with key Labour Party personnel. Some household names started to attend Labour Party Conferences. Tony Blair, the current British Prime Minister, had been creating a vision of the future based on equality, opportunity and technology. He stated that he wanted open access for all to the new technologies such as the Internet. He wanted computers in every classroom and access for every home. Anyone in the computer and communications industries would have been unwise to ignore this vision. One company, ICL, started to build strong links with key Shadow Cabinet Ministers. They were careful not to be too visible, unlike one telecommunications company, and still maintained good links with the existing Government. In September 1997, after six months of the new Administration, it was announced that ICL would be one of the key partners in the government's technology drive for education and communities.

Training and Enterprise Councils did not manage so well. The UK has 80 TECs which are government-funded organisations responsible for the delivery of youth and adult training programmes, encouraging investment in training and education and assisting in regeneration. TECs suffered from fragmentation. It was difficult for all 80 to act with one voice. It was known that Labour was concerned about the lack of public accountability, they are run mainly by local business leaders, and that they intended to rebuild regional government. Some TECs responded pre-emptatively, but generally the whole TEC movement has been experiencing months of uncertainty. In an uncertain world anticipative and courageous leadership is required. No one can afford to 'have his or her head in the sand'.

Key Influences for the Millennium

It is probable that throughout history people have thought that they were experiencing great changes. However, the rate of change in all aspects of life has never been greater than it is today. The change is not just limited to technology. All aspects of life are changing rapidly including politics, social issues and economics. Over a period of years, working with groups from all parts of the community, the author has built up a list of what may be some of the major influences for the next ten or 20 years. These are listed. Each influence presents many opportunities and threats to organisations. These have to be anticipated by those with a stake in the organisation.

Political Influences

- Greater political integration within the European Union.
- Expansion of the European Union.
- Continued pressure for governments to cut expenditure.
- Increased demand on government services particularly due to ageing populations.
- Local, national and intra-national government providing fewer services through more privatisation.
- Need to inject private investment into government services such as health and postal services.
- Tensions between centralisation and federalism e.g. strong regional government within a strong European Union.
- Governments being forced to take a more 'laissez-faire' attitude.
- Pressures for greater and less regulation.
- The continuing collapse of Communism world-wide.
- The questioning of 'hard core' Capitalism.
- More government funded Quangos (Quasi Non-governmental Organisations) and Agencies.
- The integration of left and right wing ideology into concepts such as Communitarianism.
- The tendency to move to authoritarian solutions to social problems e.g. Singapore.

Economic Influences

- Greater global free trade.
- Globalisation of supply and demand.
- Greater mobility of money.
- New employment patterns inc. more self-employment and portfolio careers.
- Emergence of low labour cost economies in the West.
- Increasing decline of relative prosperity in the West.
- Continued growth of the Pacific Rim inc. China.
- Entrenchment of trading blocks, NAFTA, EU and Asia.
- Americanisation of the globe by corporate giants in the food, film and computer industries.

Social Influences

- Breakdown of the traditional family unit.
- More single people requiring housing.
- Women emerging as the main 'bread winners'.
- Greater awareness in the diversity of staff, customers and other stakeholders.
- Greater tribalism with the increased risk of unrest and wars e.g. former Yugoslavia.
- The fragmentation of media.
- Population growth in developing nations and decline in developed nations.
- Change shock that could lead to a 'Luddite' reaction or people 'dropping out'.
- The continued growth of the 'underclass'.
- Fragmentation between those who know how to create and manipulate information and those who consume it.
- Greater spiritual diversity.
- The development of environmental stewardship.
- More mental illness.

Technical Influences

- Personalised mass-produced products.
- Recycling becomes the responsibility of the producer.
- Unlimited access to information.
- Greater standardisation with the possibility of more proliferation.

- Alternative sources of fuel.
- Major breakthroughs in health care.
- Virtual Reality.
- Bio-technology.
- Genetic Engineering.
- Rapid obsolescence.
- Continued miniaturisation of computer technology.

Each of these influences, along with the many others that exist, can present opportunities and threats to organisations and communities. Consider the fact that minority groups inc., Asian and Black people, gays and lesbians, disabled people, etc., have rightly become more vocal and confident. The opportunity to companies is that by refocusing products and services they will find new markets. This is true of the financial services companies now providing specialist investment plans for ethnic minority peoples such as West Indians. It is true for the cosmetics companies providing make up designed for black woman, who on average spend four times as much on beauty products as their white counterparts. Both the AA and RAC now make special provisions for single women whose vehicles break down. Successful companies in the future will understand that they serve highly diverse people. Of course, they should also recognise that they employ very different people and the good employers will modify their people management processes to respect this diversity. These companies will get far greater loyalty, better skills and hence better results. Companies that do not respect diversity will risk low staff morale, loss of skills, more penalties as government legislation tightens, loss of potential customers and ultimately business failure. Diversity is an issue now. It is relevant to every organisation. Ignore it at your peril. After all, as Dr Deming put it, 'survival is not compulsory'.

Process for Anticipating the Future

The most important thing is to get as much information as possible. Obviously the more people that can be involved the more information that can be gleaned. Every stakeholder of an organisation sees the news, reads the papers, listens to friends in other organisations, has a personal view, etc. This potential knowledge needs to be released.

Detailed methods for engaging stakeholders are covered in Chapter 8 of this book. The following is a summary of the process for anticipating the future.

1. Identify key stakeholders, including any relevant specialists, and decide on suitable, practical ways of involving them.

2. Gather information either directly, through facilitated brainstorms and discussions, or through indirect means such as surveys and interviews.

3. Group the issues generated using affinity or fishbone diagrams (see page 147). It is often helpful to predefine the groups such as Political, Economic, Social and Technical (PEST). Do not worry if an influence could be placed in several groups. Often influences are socio-political or have both an economic and political dimension.

4. Use techniques to prioritise the influences. Twenty percent of the influences are likely to do 80% of the influencing on the organisation in the future. Identify the critical few influences.

5. Consider each critical influence in turn and identify the respective opportunities and threats to the organisation.

6. Generate plans that can exploit the opportunities and minimise the threats.

7. Incorporate these plans into the organisation's strategic and business plans.

If this process is followed regularly and rapidly the risks of becoming remote are reduced. No one can predict the future accurately but if an organisation anticipates the future and the potential impacts it will do better than one that doesn't.

Ensuring Constancy of Purpose

The whole subject of visioning has become the butt of many jokes and stakeholders have become very wary and tired of Mission Statements. This is a shame because constancy and consistency of purpose is critical for all stakeholders of an organisation.

Dilbert cartoons abound on the subject and even situation comedies have cottoned on to the subject. The BBC, in their comedy *The Brittas Empire*, about a tragic sports centre manager, Gordon Brittas, highlighted many of the dangers of careless visioning. In a classic scene Gordon is reviewing his personal vision with his brother. Both set themselves the goals of removing illness, creating world harmony, ending wars and famine, etc. As a consequence Gordon went into leisure, to deal with the physical side of humankind and his brother joined the ministry to deal with the spiritual side. Sadly, but very amusingly, both turned out to be completely incompetent.

Where did Gordon go wrong? Firstly his aspirations, whilst noble, are somewhat unreasonable. Secondly he completely lacks any ability to inspire others. One definition of an effective leader is a person who moves towards a vision or goal and finds others following him or her. In a less ideal world it is the responsibility of the leader to facilitate the vision and to lead by example. Following some simple guidelines can help leaders avoid the meaningless platitudes that abound on company posters and in newsletters.

Guidelines for Successful Statements

It is not the statement that is the output; it is what is in stakeholders' hearts and minds. It is acting out the vision that counts, not just the words. Statements produced by small groups of leaders are notoriously unsuccessful. The key is to achieve high levels of ownership. Engaging people directly in the process can only do this. There are obvious practical constraints. A team of more than eight or ten people soon becomes ineffective, and an organisation may have thousands of stakeholders. There are, however, methods and techniques for engaging large numbers of people at one time. These will be explored in Chapter 8 and in Part 3 of this book.

The acid test is what the stakeholders feel about any statement. Do they relate to it? Does it mean anything to them on a day-to-day basis? Can they see how their jobs help achieve the purpose? Are they motivated and challenged by it? Achieving a real sense of shared purpose takes years not minutes. Without it there is the danger that everyone is trying to do his or her best without a clear aim. Dr Deming reflected on how important the aim is by stating that without it one doesn't have a system. If the goal of a leadership team is to empower its stakeholders to continuously improve all aspects of what they do (thousands of brains are always more powerful than a handful) then the absence of a shared purpose means that you run the risk of having anarchy.

Definitions

The subject is riddled with confusing and sometimes conflicting terminology. People talk about visions, aims, purposes, missions, values, principles, etc. In essence a statement of purpose is about where you want to go, what you do and what you value.

A vision or aim is the long-term ideal destination of an organisation or a key project. Where do you ideally wish to be? It should be idealistic and challenging but also attainable. As with all objective-setting approaches one starts with the end in mind and then one works back to what needs to be done on the way. It is sometimes helpful to write the vision in the present tense and to imagine what it will be like when it has been achieved. Use all your senses. What will you see, smell, hear, taste and touch. The vision should be short, memorable and meaningful. If it doesn't excite people then it is unlikely to be successful. It should not lose sight of the 'customers'.

The mission is what the organisation does. It should clearly state the scope of the organisation or project. It should not be too specific and should be flexible to handle changes in technology and other influences. Distinguish between what product you make or service you provide and what you really offer to your customers. For example a domestic appliance manufacturer does not make cookers. It provides the facility to prepare food. No one wants a cooker. They want safely prepared food. With the later mission the company should be exploring all forms of food cooking including chemical and radio wave means of heating food. Reflect on what it is that you really provide by keeping close to your customers.

The values or principles are the foundations for action. These are non-negotiable. Sacrificing values and principles may secure a short-term victory but it will usually result in a longer-term defeat. There is no such thing as value free human behaviour. In the Sixties it was trendy to talk about value-free education. This is not possible. Not valuing values is a value statement in itself. No action is devoid of values. If they are not explicit and managed there will tend to be a 'mish-mash' of the strongest individuals' beliefs. Don't commit to underpinning values unless you are very serious about enacting them in everything you do. There are too many examples of blatant hypocrisy. There is a political correctness about values and principles and everyone is producing similar wish lists. Very few organisations take their values seriously. If a core value is to invest in your staff and under the slightest pressures your first action is to 'lay off' staff don't be surprised if stakeholders become cynical. Manage values carefully.

There are some excellent examples of statements of purpose and sadly many bad ones. Some of the best are the shortest and don't include the obvious like making money. Disney is in the business of 'creating happiness'. Ritz Carlton Hotels comprise 'ladies and gentlemen serving ladies and gentlemen'. Rover cars want to supply 'baby Bentleys'. These statements conjure up positive images.

Process for Producing a Statement of Purpose

1. Decide which stakeholders need to be actively involved.
2. Select an appropriate method. Small-scale sessions are easier to manage and cheaper, but they do not get the ownership that comes from large-scale events.
3. Explain to all those involved the benefits of having such a discussion.
4. Use brainstorming and grouping techniques to get everyone generating key words or short statements.
5. Distinguish between vision, mission and values.
6. Rationalise into a statement or statements and review.
7. Record any other issues that come out of the session.

Some organisations, particularly schools, have started to use art and drama to help children in visioning. This is very successful but may not be appropriate in other environments.

Constancy of purpose is critical. Try to put aside any prejudices about the subject and ensure that there is high stakeholder ownership. The results will take time to achieve but will be worthwhile. We have probably all experienced the difference of working for an organisation that is vision-less and one that knows where it is going and everyone is pulling in the same direction.

Identifying Critical Success Factors

Vision without method is futile and frustrating. Method without vision is direction-less. There has to be a link from the statement of purpose, the anticipation of the future and the customers' wants and needs into concrete action. Critical Success Factors are the link from the future into the present.

Any factor that is critical to the achievement of future success is defined as a Critical Success Factor or CSF. CSFs provide the means of linking what people do with he future intentions. They are the pre-requisites for success. So far in the strategic planning process the stakeholders have concentrated externally, on customers and competition, and on the future, through anticipation and vision. Now they need to look internally. What are the outcomes, or groups of outcomes, which if not achieved will jeopardise the whole strategy?

Ownership of CSFs is very important and so engaging stakeholders in their production is essential. All stakeholders need to be clear about the CSFs, so a list that is short is ideal. The Unit within the Royal Air Force that had several pages of CSFs was destined to struggle. Staff could not possibly relate to them on a day-to-day basis without picking up the gargantuan strategic plan. CSFs should be succinct, well defined and meaningful. CSFs will interrelate and sometimes it can be difficult to make them discrete.

Typical Critical Success Factors

There appears to be some fairly generic CSFs for all types of organisation. The Business Excellence Model (see Figure 11) gives a clue as to their extent. However, the process of arriving at the short-list is just as important as the list itself. Using a predefined list is unlikely to get high levels of stakeholder ownership. For this reason it is usually best to start from 'a clean piece of paper'.

Typical Critical Success Factors for a School

- Sound, flexible teaching and learning methods.
- Broad, balanced, relevant curriculum.
- Effective leadership and management.
- Strong pastoral care.
- Highly skilled and motivated staff inc. teaching and support staff.
- Adequate financial resources used prudently.
- Positive interaction with the wider community.
- Clean, safe environment.
- Strong parental support.

Typical Critical Success Factors for a Manufacturing Company

- Effective financial controls.
- Long-term supplier partnerships.
- Highly skilled and motivated workforce.
- Rapid turnaround time for new and improved products and services.
- Short lead times.
- Innovative and proven designs.
- Capable production processes.
- Understanding of customers' existing and future wants and needs.

Apart from being stated in the language of success, CSFs should also be outcomes or achievements. They may well cover internal as well as external factors.

Process for defining and agreeing Critical Success Factors

1. Decide which stakeholders need to be actively involved.
2. Select an appropriate method for engagement.
3. Review customers' wants and needs, competitor analysis, future influences and statement of purpose.
4. Brainstorm all the factors for success.
5. Group these using an Affinity or Fishbone Diagram (see page 147).
6. Agree labels for the groupings, ensuring that these are positive outcomes.
7. Review whether the grouping is critical or not. A factor is critical if its absence jeopardises the achievement of future success.
8. Review each CSF and ensure that the definition is clear.
9. Record the CSFs and circulate to other stakeholders for comment.

Critical Success Factors start to convert the future into today's priorities. Clarity of definition and ownership are important to make them useful. The next stage is to link these results to actions.

Prioritising and Aligning Processes

Much has already been written in this book about the importance of process. Processes are the means by which work gets done. They are highly interdependent and often very complex. Processes can be analysed at any level. For the purpose of strategic planning it is important to 'map' the highest level, or key, processes. The highest level map should show how the organisation fits with its key stakeholders. This will involve producing a model of the 'community' into which the organisation fits. Examples of these types of model are shown in Part 3 of the book. Once the community-wide model is produced, a model of the organisation's key processes can be created.

The purpose of this stage of the strategic planning process is to highlight the critical processes. These are the processes that if improved, or in some cases even created, will produce the greatest strategic result. As previously stated, 20% of the activity can produce up to 80% of the strategic intent. It is important to focus activity on the critical few not the trivial many.

It is important at this stage to distinguish between action and reaction. It is impossible to work on an outcome or CSF. One can only modify a process and then observe the impact on the CSF/s. Improvement activity should be grounded in sound theory and not just on manic hunches. Tools exist that highlight the possible and actual links between actions and reactions. Because the interrelationships can be complete, a simple two-dimensional matrix or table can be used. Along the top of the table are listed the results, reactions or CSFs. Down the left-hand side of the table are listed the activities or key processes. A group can then discuss whether improving a process is likely to have a strong, medium or weak impact on the CSFs or even no impact at all. The matrix or table can then be used to highlight critical processes in need of improvement or even critical processes that are so weak that they are barely present. One school completing this stage discovered they it had virtually no processes to achieve strong links with local employers. The CSF was just an idle wish.

Process for Prioritising and Aligning Processes

1. Decide which stakeholders need to be actively involved.
2. Select an appropriate method for engagement.
3. Using process-modelling tools, produce a view of how the organisation interrelates with all its key stakeholders.

4. Use the same modelling tools to produce a high level model of the organisation's key processes.

5. Fill in a table or matrix with CSFs along the top and key processes down the left-hand side.

6. Considering each process in turn, discuss and agree the likely impact on the CSFs of improving this process. Fill in the rows with symbols representing strong, medium or weak impacts. If there is no perceived impact leave the field blank.

7. From the matrix list the processes in order of criticality.

8. Identify any gaps i.e., CSFs with no contributing processes.

9. Discuss the results and agree the final priorities.

Organisations have too little time to waste 'moving the deckchairs on the Titanic'. This strategic planning process is offered as a means of identifying the improvement priorities. No model is perfect and it has its limitations. The many organisations that have used this approach have tended to improve it every time. They have recognised the need to continually improve the critical process — strategic planning.

Chapter 7

Engaging Stakeholders in Process Improvement

To achieve long-term systemic improvement, people have to be engaged in continually improving processes in which they have a stake. Process improvement is much more than problem solving. A process does not have to be failing to be improved. It is important, however, to focus limited time and energy on improving important or critical processes.

Improvement Cycles

If stakeholders are going to be engaged they need to follow a structured approach to improvement. Such a structure gives direction and avoids wasteful digressions. Contrary to popular perception, a flexible structure encourages innovation.

There are many such improvement cycles. Many organisations, including the Royal Mail and Rank Xerox, have developed their own. Some are excessively complex, others too simplistic. The most universal is the Shewart Cycle mentioned earlier: Plan, Do, Study, Act (PDSA). This covers the planning of a potential improvement, its implementation and reflection on how successful it has been. If no improvement has occurred, or the process has deteriorated, then some things have been learnt and theories can be revised accordingly. If successful, the result needs to be acted upon by implementing it throughout the process or in similar processes.

The cycle in this book focuses throughout on process. The Shewart Cycle is incorporated in the improvement stage. The three stages are: define the process, analyse the process and finally improve the process (Figure 13). The plethora of tools and techniques can then be linked to the cycle, so the stakeholders know when to apply which tool. It is important that the cycle be started at 'Define'. The first part of this step is defining the task. This must be done before any improvement work is carried out. If the cycle is being applied to an existing process then it should be followed in a clockwise direction, each step being successfully completed before the next is started.

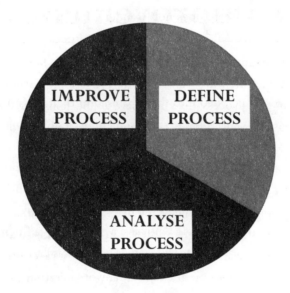

Figure 13. The Process Improvement Cycle

Define a Process and Plan its Improvement

Four elements need to be defined at this stage. These are the task, the team, the process and the plan.

Task

The team requires a clearly defined task, which has been agreed by all the relevant stakeholders. This objective should specify the expected results of the improvement initiative and the means by which success will be judged. It should also include the reasons for the task and any other relevant background information.

At this stage in the improvement process it is not possible to be too specific because thorough analysis has not been completed. The objective must not anticipate specific solutions but it should clearly identify the process to be investigated. It should also clarify how much the team has been empowered. Is the team expected to produce recommendations or are they to proceed to piloting and full-scale implementation? What are the mechanisms for reporting and gaining further support if required?

The task, which is documented in the statement of objective, must be regularly reviewed to ensure that the team does not 'wander'. It may be necessary for the task to be refined or revised throughout the improvement process.

Team

If the process to be improved is core to the organisation then a team will be required. Individuals as well as teams can apply the improvement cycle. Teams need to be correctly constituted and well facilitated. The cost of running ineffective teams is very high.

The team needs to be representative of the different stakeholders of the process being improved. It might be necessary for the person who is establishing the team to produce a rough process map in order to identify, the customers, suppliers, process owners and operators and other people who have a controlling influence. These groups should be represented on the core team. It may be relevant to include information technology and finance specialists.

There is a tension between representation and team size. The optimum size of a working team is between six and ten people. In order to ensure thorough stakeholder representation it may be possible to have people represent more than one group. Otherwise different means of getting them involved may have to be considered such as questionnaires or special sessions.

Some organisations use personality models such as Belbin and Myers Briggs to ensure psychological, as well as stakeholder diversity. Others rely more on chance and look for enthusiastic, knowledgeable volunteers.

The team needs to decide on the frequency and duration of meetings. Typically these vary from Quality Circle type meetings, which last for an hour a week, through to full time Re-engineering Teams (see 'Improve a Process'), which may exist for months or even years. There are many options in between these extremes.

Once constituted the team needs to be well-facilitated using sound meeting management techniques. A code of co-operation, established by the team, is important in defining the way in which they wish to work. The first action of the team is to review and agree the task.

Process

The majority of causes of variation come from the process not the individual. Therefore process understanding is central to achieving real, sustainable improvement. Except in special cases the improvement team should focus on the process not the individuals who carry out the process. People in manufacturing would not be allowed to tamper with a production process unless they understood it well. Non-manufacturing processes can be less visible but offer enormous potential for improvement. The team must understand the context in which the current process operates, and particularly for whom, prior to starting analysis. Process modelling tools enable the team to share a basic understanding of the process.

The necessary degree of understanding varies according to the strategy for improvement. If quantum, dramatic improvements are desired, as in process re-engineering, then little more than a simple definition is required. If more gradual improvements are desired then the process will need to be understood in detail using process models and flowcharts.

In all cases the process must be defined in order to understand who the customers are, along with their ideal wants and needs. The customers may be internal and external to the organisation. This kind of analysis prevents much embarrassment later in the improvement cycle by forcing the team to answer the 'obvious' questions.

Plan

The team needs to produce an outline plan. At this stage in the cycle this will be quite general including the estimated duration of the work and key milestones. Teams usually use the improvement cycle as a structure e.g., define step — complete in four weeks, analyse in four months and improve in six months. It is not possible to be too specific because the team cannot predict the results of their analysis work.

Analyse a Process

Effective analysis of the existing process comprises three stages: measurement and identifying and prioritising the key issues.

Measure

The 'critical few' measures can be identified from the definition of the process. The team should start with what is important to measure, not what is easy. They should strive to measure the performance of the existing process but recognise that some of the most important information may be 'unknown or unknowable'.

'Hard' measures generate numerical data. This quantitative information must be accompanied by the definition which was used in its generation. A definition is classified as operational if it is useful and shared by the stakeholders. Softer, qualitative information may be useful but, like hard measures, it should be used cautiously. 'Soft' information would cover perceptions, beliefs and attitudes.

Ultimately management by visible figures alone may be one of Western management's deadly diseases (52). Measurement, which is not based on solid understanding, can be very harmful. There are many powerful measurement tools.

Identify Issues

A process does not have to be failing in order to be improved. Process improvement is much more than just problem solving. A process may have been selected for improvement because it is central to the organisation's future strategy, because of its potential impact on customer satisfaction and other key success factors or because it is currently failing to perform.

In the traditional area of problem solving the team needs to distinguish between cause and effect. Root causes have a tendency to be far away in distance and time from the symptoms. An apparently minor 'ripple' in one part of the process may lead to a 'tidal wave' further 'downstream'. Techniques such as fishbone diagrams and relation diagrams are used to distinguish root causes from symptoms.

In a more proactive situation an improvement team may be trying to identify improvement opportunities. These could be gradual or dramatic but they enable the process to perform at a higher level than present, even if this appears adequate for the time being. In this situation the team is not exploring root causes of problems but constraints to improvement. These constraints can be analysed in a similar way to root causes.

Prioritise

Once potential issues have been identified these have to be prioritised. All organisations have limited resources. Therefore improvement teams need to work smart not just hard. Through careful prioritisation teams can get the maximum benefit from the minimum effort. Twenty percent of the root causes of a problem, lead to 80% of the effect. Twenty percent of the constraints to improvement, if removed, could generate 80% of the benefits.

Improve a Process

There are seven stages to improving a process, incorporating the PDSA cycle.

Generate Possible Improvements

Now that issues have been identified and prioritised the team can move into generating as many improvements as possible. The aim at this stage is to encourage divergent, creative thinking. The team should consider several different improvement strategies. They include corrective and preventive action as well as more proactive gradual or dramatic improvements.

If the process has failed to perform to existing standards then it is likely that corrective action will be required. Corrections are still a cost of failure but may be justified in their own right. Spending a hundred pounds to rectify a problem that could cost thousands and jeopardise reputation with customers is well worthwhile.

Once a corrective action has been taken time should be allocated to decide whether a preventive action is required and particularly whether the process needs to be fundamentally improved. Often organisations are so caught up in 'fire-fighting' that they think that they do not have the time to investigate preventing recurrence of problems. If they do not make this investment then chances are they will carry on reacting to these problems until they do.

A preventive action has to address the real roots of the problem rather than the symptoms. It may take time but the investment will be returned many times over.

Other more proactive improvement strategies cover improving the process in the absence of problems. Whether this is economic will depend on the specific process, available technology and the overall loss to society, not just for the provider of the product or service but for all the other stakeholders too. Assuming improvement is viable there are two distinct approaches: Kaizen and Re-engineering.

Kaizen is based on the premise of improving the existing process gradually but forever. Over time the results can be very impressive. It is analogous to 'the pennies saving the pounds' and involves all stakeholders. It was the cornerstone of the Japanese economic miracle, started in the Fifties. Leading Japanese companies are obsessed with finding improvements all the time. Suggestion schemes generate fantastic volumes of ideas, many of which are implemented.

If a process is fundamentally constrained or so far behind its competitors in performance then Kaizen may take too long or may not address the real issues. In this case the improvement team may need to explore the principles of Re-engineering. This approach is based on looking for dramatic, quantum improvements by challenging all preconceived ideas. The risk of failure is greater than Kaizen but then the rewards can be much greater too. A key to Re-engineering is to look for opportunities everywhere not just in technology but also in changes in political, social and economic circumstances.

In practice it is often difficult to distinguish precisely what type of improvement is occurring. In the end the team wants to maximise benefits so it should explore all opportunities. It is possible that the team started by addressing a problem and in the improvement stage identified a re-engineering opportunity.

The key is to encourage creativity and not to be constrained by the team's own view of the way things are. These preconceptions are often referred to as paradigms and they often block us from innovation. A passing comment could be the start of a great new idea and this is why it is so important to get the right chemistry in the improvement team.

Select

Once many possible improvement actions have been generated they need to be rationalised. Some ideas may be patently unworkable, but be careful about 'group think' and paradigms. Others may contain interesting themes or concepts.

The remaining ideas can be grouped. They can then be prioritised using techniques such as paired comparison and weighted selection (see pages 149 and 151). If there are several favoured solutions it may be possible to hybrid them, thus getting the best out of all the alternatives. At the end of this stage the team is likely to have a short-list of practical improvements ready to be considered in more detail.

Design and Plan

It is likely that no more than two or three improvements will be taken into this stage at any one time. Firstly the improvement needs to be designed in detail. Improvements may vary from minor changes to major process redesigns.

Once the desired improvement has been designed a plan needs to be produced to implement it. Planning techniques such as Tree Diagrams and Critical Path Analysis (see pages 135 and 138) may be used to sequence and schedule activities.

A key decision is whether to pilot the change or to implement it more widely. This will depend on the team's confidence but it is generally advisable to pilot improvements first. The team also needs to consider possible resistance to the implementation of these changes. Many, technically fine solutions have come unstuck at this stage because some of the deeper, psychological reasons for resisting change were not predicted and designed out.

Implement

Once the improvements have been planned they can be implemented. If the team has been successful there should be little resistance and the implementation should proceed according to plan. If deviations do occur the team should be prepared to take corrective action.

Study

Once the implementation is complete the team can study the results to see if their predictions were correct. If successful they will proceed to the next stage. If unsuccessful they must revise their theories. 'Failing forward' is fine and the team should not become despondent. Failure is an inherent part of innovation and learning. In this situation the team may need to go back to Define or Analyse and question their assumptions. This kind of honest innovation will only happen where people are safe to fail and this culture will only be created if fear is driven out of the organisation. A fearful culture is not a creative one.

Communicate

The results of the improvement team's work do need to be communicated to other stakeholders. Much can be learnt from failure as well as from success. The key here is to prevent duplication of effort and to encourage learning, not copying, from each other.

Proceduralise

If the pilot improvement has been successful then the team should consider repeating it throughout the rest of the process and in other similar processes throughout the organisation.

Any successful improvements should be included in the relevant procedures. Some of the tools used throughout the improvement cycle can be used as visual procedures to reduce the dependence on text. By using the same tools for quality assurance as for process improvement a large amount of time and effort can be saved. The process improvement cycle automatically generates a lot of material that forms the basis of procedures.

Chapter 8

Methods, Tools and Techniques for Engaging Stakeholders

The terms methods, tools and techniques are often used interchangeably. For the purpose of this section they are defined as follows. A method is an overall, step-by-step approach that utilises both tools and techniques. Both the strategic planning process, in Chapter 6, and the process improvement cycle, in Chapter 7, are methods. A technique is less broad in scope than a method. A technique comprises a range of tools such as large group techniques. A tool is a very specific mechanism for achieving a well-defined task such as using a Fishbone Diagram for cause and effect analysis. In summary a method uses a range of techniques and techniques, comprise tools.

Consultants and academics generally agree on methods. They often disagree strongly over techniques and tools. This is a shame because the choice of techniques and tools will depend on practical issues such as desired accuracy, available time, the number of stakeholders to be involved, cost, etc. All organisations and projects need to apply strategic planning and continual process improvement. All techniques and tools have strengths and limitations. There is no single 'Holy Grail'.

Methods

Two methods have already been explored in detail. The first is for engaging stakeholders in strategic planning. The second is for engaging stakeholders in process improvement. There may well be other methods but it is felt that these two are comprehensive. The strategic planning process covers aspects of planning for the future and identifying critical processes. The process improvement cycle embraces aspects of marketing and incorporates the Plan, Do, Study Act cycle which is founded on continual evaluation. The improvement cycle can be applied to delivery processes such as production, teaching, nursing, etc., as well as to support processes such as recruitment, training, resource deployment and strategic planning itself.

Techniques

Improvement Teams

Successful quality improvement does not just depend on the effective application of the tools. Just as important is an effective team. This means that practical psychology needs to be considered and applied.

A major restriction to quality improvement is fear. In a fearful environment innovation and risk taking will be very rare. The desired environment is one that is supporting and nurturing. It must be based on an obsession to learn. Teams should have access to best practice, whether through magazines, books, videos, networking and visits. 'Re-inventing the wheel' should be avoided but just because no one has done it before should not be a reason for not trying.

The environment must allow for honest failure. Failure can be a valid learning experience. 'Failing forward' is perfectly acceptable and required if continual improvement is to be achieved. If the team is going to pass through failure, tenacity becomes an important team and individual attribute.

The team must be secure in order to be honest with each other. Hidden agendas and selfish ambitions should be avoided or exposed. Competition within the team carries great risks. Competition should be encouraged with real competitors not between internal staff and other stakeholders.

It is essential to involve the right people in the improvement initiative. Successful implementation depends on ownership. A person does not own an initiative unless they have been involved in its development. Broad stakeholder representation dramatically reduces conflict, which in turn reduces implementation time and can ultimately prevent failure. It also encourages innovation by minimising 'group think'.

The team members must reflect the correct expertise to contribute to improvement. To decide who should be on the team, it helps to produce a process model or flowchart. Any organisation or department, which is part of the process, should be represented. The downside to this is that effective teams should not be more than ten persons, so other approaches for involvement may be required.

It is important that each member of the team knows his or her responsibilities. There are several key roles to be filled. The first is that of Team Leader. This person will be responsible for guiding and directing the team towards their objectives. He or she will also have to monitor progress and initiate corrective action if required. The team will probably need the services of a Facilitator. This is someone proficient in the use of the tools and techniques. Ideally all leaders should be proficient Facilitators. Facilitators need to be truly impartial, directing the proceedings but not the outcomes. There may be merit in having an external Facilitator who is not too close to the process being improved. In the team someone needs to agree to be Administrator. He/she will plan meetings and produce and circulate agendas and minutes. If the team is operating in a large organisation, or has many different organisations represented, then it is advisable to have a Champion. This person is usually non-executive but is of a status to unblock any political problems that the team may encounter. The Champion can also help secure funds along with monitoring the progress of the team.

In situations where it is impossible to involve representatives from all stakeholders it may be necessary to second people onto the team for a limited period. Another idea is to arrange a special event where a stakeholder group can be involved in a 'one off' activity such as a brainstorm.

The next issue is resourcing. How frequently is the team going to meet and for how long? For multi-organisational improvement teams it is impractical to meet once a week so these teams tend to meet for longer less frequently. This may be three hours every three weeks or for half a day per month. The same applies to internal teams that are tackling very complex processes. In these cases an hour a week barely enables the team to go into any depth. These teams often also choose to meet less frequently but for longer.

In order to monitor progress it is important to have a Quality Steering Group or Forum. This team helps prioritise improvement initiatives and acts as a watchdog. The most immediate form of monitoring comes from the Leader. If problems cannot be resolved and the team redirected, then the Champion and Steering Group may need to be involved. The main monitoring is against the objectives produced and agreed by the team. The Leader should also monitor softer issues such as morale and motivation and take action accordingly. In all monitoring, care should be taken to avoid creating fear. Monitoring and appraisal should be done in a positive, non-threatening, way.

Once the team has met the objectives it should be concluded with a final review and recognition for achievements should be given.

Improvement Teams generate very high levels of ownership for the people involved. They are often responsible for completing the whole improvement cycle, right through to achievement of results. If the team is correctly constituted, with broad stakeholder representation, it is more likely to challenge the status quo and generate innovative solutions. Because the team members will be working together over a potentially long period they are more likely to develop meaningful relationships which will benefit day-to-day operation.

It is very de-motivating for the team if the traditional leadership structure overrides team suggestions. Some leaders find the process too time consuming and would rather resort to the command and control style of leadership. The main limitation of improvement teams is their maximum size. This can lead to imbalances of power between the stakeholders.

Open Space Technology

Harrison Owen is widely recognised as the main proponent and developer of Open Space Technology (OST). It is a very loosely structured approach for engaging very large numbers of stakeholders. The largest session has involved 2000 people in an aircraft hanger! 'OST is effective in situations where a diverse group of people must deal with complex, and potentially conflicting material, in innovative and productive ways'. (53) It should not be used when someone in power thinks that they know the answer or in situations where people in traditional leadership roles are 'control freaks'.

The technique is founded on some clear and proven principles. It is designed to encourage passion and responsibility. Those who need to be present to get the job done are invited. No one is 'press ganged'. Whoever cares will attend. These people are encouraged to stay for the whole process, which can last from one hour to three days maximum. OST has been designed in a similar way to the Market Places used by Africans and Native Americans. The checklist for running OST includes:

- Appropriateness — is OST the appropriate technique?
- Theme — is the theme clearly focused but flexible to allow for innovation?
- Time — has enough time been allocated?
- Main Space — is the main space large enough for all participants to sit in concentric cycles and to feel comfortable?
- The Wall — is there a suitably large wall to act as the focal point for the 'Market Place'?
- Other Spaces — are there suitable spaces or rooms for the groups to work in?
- Food and Drink — is food and drink available and flexible throughout the process?
- Supplies — are there adequate supplies of Post It Notes™, flipchart paper, masking tape, etc.?
- Venue — can the staff of the venue cope with such an event?

The Facilitator initiates the process. He or she states the theme, describes the process, creates the bulletin board and opens the Market Place. People are then asked to identify issues and opportunities related to the theme. They come into the centre of the circle, state their name and issue, record both on a piece of paper and tape it onto the wall. They then return to their seat in the circle. This process of generating issues and opportunities proceeds as along as is necessary. The Facilitator then schedules the issues into typically two-hour time slots. There are a number of breakout spaces and so many issues can be handled concurrently. Participants then 'sign up' to sessions. They can negotiate to have sessions rescheduled or combined but this has to be done with the consent of the person who raised the issue in the first place.

Now the Market Place starts for real. The people who raised the issues have to agree to facilitate and record the discussions. The 'law of two feet' operates for the other participants. This states that if at any point in the discussion a person finds that they are neither learning nor contributing they can go to a more productive place. This is a great way to dis-empower the megalomaniacs or those who like the sound of their own voices. In this way the participants decide the priorities. At the end of the process the records of the discussions are collated. If there is enough time and technology the OST report can be produced in 'real time'. According to Owen the ultimate facilitator will do nothing and remain totally invisible. Their job is to create and hold the space for the participants.

There are some very exciting features to OST. The first is the complete freedom for stakeholders to contribute. The process is not technocratic and is self-regulating. Another key feature, sometimes lost in brainstorming, is that the person who raises the issue has to take responsibility for it. Owen has certainly had some interesting results but does this process lead to long-term behavioural changes and sustainable results? The process makes no distinction between root causes and symptoms and is not very data driven. As Owen states it is certainly not for those who like control but it can work with very diverse groups of stakeholders.

Future Search

Marvin Weisbord and Sandra Janoff have developed a more structured approach. This is called Future Search. It has been used widely throughout the USA. In the UK it is being linked to Agenda 21 work. This came out of the Rio Conference on the global environment. Agenda 21 aims to engage communities in developing sustainable solutions to their problems such as transport.

Future Search events usually involve 60 to 70 stakeholders. There are five main tasks.
29

1. Review the past.
2. Explore the present.
3. Create ideal future scenarios.
4. Identify common ground.
5. Make action plans.

Experience has shown that it is best to involve stakeholders at all the stages of planning, doing and reviewing. A group will form a steering committee to ensure that all the conditions for success are met.

Weisbord has summarised the learning assumptions underpinning the Future Search technique as follows (54).

Each person:

- Has a unique learning style.
- Learns at a different rate.
- Learn different things from a common experience.
- Learns best from his or her experience.
- Learns more in one conference than the world will let us apply.
- Has the ability to help and teach others.
- Benefits from trial, error and feedback.

These are very sound and comprehensive principles.

Reviewing the past involves all participants identifying personal, global and organisational events they have experienced within a certain period of time. These events are pasted onto a large notice board covered in a strip of paper. Coloured dots are used to highlight the important events.

Focusing on the present starts with mind-mapping the group's perceptions of external trends that are currently shaping their lives and organisations. This exercise is then continued in stakeholder groups. Finally, each stakeholder group identifies things that are proud of and things that they are sorry about. Each step in this process is concluded with large group reviews and discussions.

Now the participants are ready to focus on the future. They are asked to put themselves ten to 20 years into the future and to imagine and act out the future as if it were now. Common future themes are recorded along with potential projects and unresolved differences.

Next the group reviews the lists and makes sure that they all agree what is meant. The process concludes with the formulation and presentation of long and short-term plans. Opportunities are created for collaboration and for working across boundaries.

The whole process is run over three days. The agenda is synchronised so that reflection happens overnight. Ground rules or a code of co-operation are established at the start.

One of the greatest strengths of Future Search is the reflection on the past. It is said that you cannot know where you are going unless you understand where you have been. It also sets local issues firmly in national and even global frameworks. Like Open Space Technology a lot of effort is placed on creating the right physical environment. Compared to OST Future Search is quite structured and directly facilitated. Perhaps the safe environment is more important than the exact technique or tools used.

Scenario Planning

Scenario planning is not a new concept. It has been in use in some industries for many years. More recently some people have started to apply it to community-wide issues. Public Voice International, co-ordinated by Karl Berger and Matthew Pike, has been in the vanguard in the UK. Questionably the best example of scenario planning took place in the mid-Eighties in Chattanooga, USA. PVI invests a lot of time developing the scenarios with the stakeholders. The more care taken with the scenarios, the better the result.

One such project called 'Choices for Britain' was developed in partnership with the then Avon Local Education Authority. PVI worked closely with teachers and advisers to develop four possible scenarios for Great Britain. These included trying to retain a global presence, taking a stronger, more integrated approach in Europe or modelling ourselves along the lines of Sweden, investing more in diversity and environment. These scenarios were written up into a very professional pack of materials designed to appeal to students. The content of the material was also designed to be compatible with the UK's National Curriculum. In this way it met the teachers' requirements as well as the students' wants and needs. Teachers who used the pack discussed and debated each scenario with classes of students. Students then decided on their own priorities and 'voted' for the favoured options. The results were then presented back to other key players such as Local Councillors and the Training and Enterprise Council. Of key concern to the young people were the environment and inclusive communities.

Funds were then obtained to run a 'Choices for Bristol' Project. In the same way scenarios were prepared with stakeholders. These were then published in a local newspaper. People were encouraged to form their own discussion groups based on geography or particular issues. The results of their discussions were submitted to a voluntary co-ordinating body that was located in a City Council location. No concepts and ideas were excluded. A summary of the results was taken 'on the road' to key venues for people to review and add to. Finally, several facilitated sessions were organised for people to come and prioritise the issues and to arrive at an overall vision. Several improvement projects were subsequently formed to provide continuity.

'Choices for Bristol' struggled in many ways. There were a low number of contributions from a small number of people. This gave politicians the chance to argue that it was not representative of the community as a whole. Political infighting amongst the 'power brokers' led to uncertainty, and the departure of the project manager before the start of the process was very unsettling. However, valuable lessons were learnt and the information fed back to all the key agencies.

Scenario planning struggles in one or two areas. It is not truly 'free wheeling' because the scenarios are prepared in advance. Also the stakeholders do not actually all come together at the same time. If the number of people participating is low then the results can easily be discounted or special interest groups can have too much influence. Accessibility is an issue. Can people with other commitments, like jobs and children, and disabled people actually get to attend? Its greatest strength lies in enabling people, who may have been systematically disempowered, to see that there are alternative futures and that they may be able to influence them.

Large Scale Facilitated Workshops

General McArther introduced Dr Deming, Dr Juran and Homer Sarasohn to Japanese business leaders just after the Second World War. Since then Japanese companies have developed their teachings on quality management into a fine art. The Japanese often refer to this as Total Quality Control. The West discovered these concepts in the early Eighties and called them Total Quality Management (TQM). Business led the application of TQM but it was not long until the Public Sector and more recently whole communities started to experiment with the principles, tools and techniques.

Many of the tools and techniques of TQM work best in small teams of no more than ten people. As it became necessary to engage larger numbers of stakeholders other ways of facilitating had to be developed. One such approach is large-scale facilitated workshops. These have much in common with the previous techniques.

The process is only used where the answer is not known and barriers need to be broken down. The lead facilitator makes it clear that he or she is not going to influence the outcome, only guide the process to ensure that there is a satisfactory outcome for the majority of stakeholders. Considerable time is invested with the stakeholders to design an appropriate approach based on Profound Knowledge and using the tools of Total Quality. This is not taken 'off the shelf' but is always tailored to the clients' individual wants and needs. To date numbers involved have ranged from 30 to 200. Teamwork is always done in groups of ten. Volunteers act as facilitators during the events and are trained 'just in time' and coached by the lead facilitator. Events are rarely more than two days in duration.

At the start of the event the whole group prepares a Code of Co-operation which they agree to adhere to and to 'police'. This gives permission for participants and facilitators to highlight breaches safely, when they occur. Often a Force Field Analysis (see page 133) is done to highlight what is really driving the work and what might restrain it. The detailed agenda and tools used will depend on the theme. Work is usually done in mixed stakeholder groups although it may be appropriate at certain stages not to mix. Key questions are usually raised and answered using the tools. These include: who are the customers, what are their wants and needs, what is the process, where are the barriers, what are the root cause issues, what creative solutions can be used to resolve them, how can we work together to make sure we resolve them? Continual review and evaluation is carried out with the facilitators as well as the other participants. Facilitators are trained and briefed in the first hour of the event and supported throughout the process by the lead facilitator. At the end of each day the facilitators have a de-briefing which includes lessons learnt and how to approach further work.

Many such sessions have been run with very diverse groups. The process has much strength, not least of all getting the participants to concentrate on process and away from blaming people. They also learn new skills and tools that they can apply personally. It is more structured than OST to allow rapid feedback. Real time reports are produced and some sessions opt to have a multi-media record on CD-ROM. These techniques do not dwell on the past as much as Future Search ones. The main constraint is that some people find the tools too technical. This can be minimised if they are used covertly but other tools such as art and drama are being considered.

Overall Conclusions on Techniques

People tend to get very possessive about 'their' favoured techniques. Perhaps they have more in common then at first appears. The underlying principles are more important than the technique or tool itself. There are certain pre-requisites for all of the techniques described in this book.

- All stakeholders must be actively involved.
- All people must have physical and mental access.
- Work on the process. Do not blame people.
- Get to the root causes.
- Build peoples' confidence.
- Believe in what people have to offer and show respect.
- Avoid excessive structure.
- Have no prepared outcomes or 'right answers'.
- Encourage innovation and creativity.
- Build relationships.
- Ensure continuity.
- Do not hide from complexity.
- Use data cautiously and respect feelings and perceptions.
- Use suitable environments.

Tools

The majority of the tools summarised in the next part of the book, along with many others not covered, are explained in far greater detail in the Quality Toolkit (55). This book is designed around the improvement cycle. Each tool has a purpose, principles, a method for practical application, guidelines, examples drawn from all types of organisation and proformas where applicable.

In this book the tools are grouped by their main purpose eg. planning, process modelling, consensus, etc.

Tools for Planning

Force Field Analysis

Force Field Analysis enables the deeper motivations for change to be explored. It helps make sense of the status quo and can be used to prevent or minimise conflict. It is applied in situations where there are pressures to change. The forces driving change are identified as well as the forces restraining change. The idea is to develop strategies which build on the drivers and reduce or remove the restraints.

All organisations tend to resist change. Understanding the status quo and the real motivations helps in facilitating change. Force Field Analysis addresses the psychology of change. Its apparent simplicity should not lead people to underestimate its usefulness. Many technically superb improvements have failed to see the light of day because of lack of attention to the less tangible issues. An example of Force Field Analysis is shown in Figure 14.

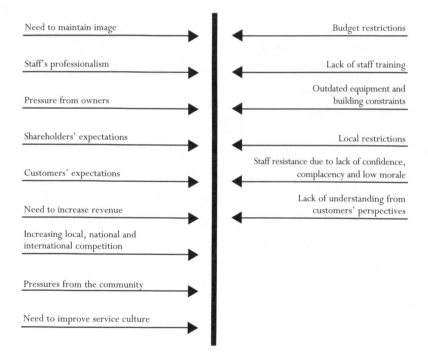

Figure 14. Example of Force Field Analysis for improving quality in an hotel

Critical Path Analysis

Critical Path Analysis is a planning technique for major projects. Activities are sequenced and their duration estimated. This enables planners to predict completion dates, to carry out 'what if' investigations, to improve their plan and to monitor progress throughout the project. Planning is made more effective by the identification of the critical path. Activities on the critical path, if allowed to slip, will delay the achievement of the whole project. Focusing on critical path activities leads to better use of time and to improvements, which may bring completion dates forward.

Critical Path Analysis is one of the techniques within a portfolio of planning techniques referred to as the Programme Evaluation and Review Technique or PERT for short. Other techniques include Gantt Charts and resource balancing techniques, which use bar charts. All of these techniques are based on the Logical Constraints Map. This is the diagram which shows the logical sequences of the tasks. It has to be produced before the critical path can be identified. Tasks or activities can be logically constrained. They may also be constrained by resources but this is not considered at the early stages of planning.

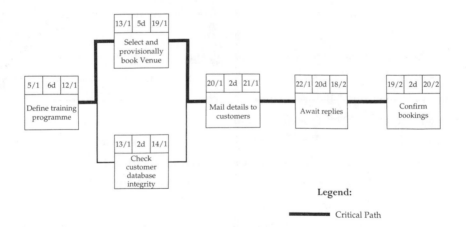

Figure 15. Example of a Critical Path Analysis for oganising a Training Course

Consider the example of a mailshot. The task of printing the mailers would have to be complete before the envelopes could be 'stuffed'. In this case the tasks have to be done in series i.e., printing before 'stuffing'. One has to be complete before the other can start. Preparing the mailing list, however, could be done at the same time as the printing of the mailer. In this case the activities are in parallel. All the tasks need to be laid out showing their logical links with each other. This is the Logical Constraints Map.

A project has a distinct start and finish. Processes tend to be continuous. All processes will be preceded by a project to implement and commission the process. Project planning techniques, such as Critical Path Analysis, have time as one of their dimensions. Process modelling techniques show feedback. Planning ones do not because it is not yet possible to go back in time. An example of a Critical Path Analysis is shown in Figure 15.

Benchmarking

Benchmarking is a structured approach for comparing the products, services and processes of an organisation against the world's best. It raises expectations, identifies gaps in current performance and may lead to ideas for improvement. In essence benchmarking is about finding and implementing best practice.

An organisation can benchmark a product, a service, a process or the whole organisation. The term benchmark originates from bench tests that were done with computer products to compare their performance. Manufacturers now also use benchmarking to compare the processes that produce the products.

The key to successful benchmarking is knowing your own organisation before seeking to change it. Before beginning your improvement efforts, current performance must be carefully analysed. Only through detailed local understanding of processes can you begin to identify the performance gap that exists between yourself and higher performers and what action is required to achieve the change. Benchmarking is about identifying processes that work better elsewhere and, if appropriate, emulating them.

Benchmarking can be competitive or non-competitive. League tables promote the concept of benchmarking between competing organisations. Alternatively an organisation could benchmark against a non-competitor that is highly regarded in the service or process being investigated. Examples would include world-class private sector organisations and the best practitioners in the public sector. The choice will depend on what is being benchmarked.

Non-competitive benchmarking tends to be collaborative. Some competitors are even starting to introduce this style of approach, realising the limitations of outright competition and the potential benefits to all parties of sharing certain information.

Competitive benchmarking should be based on direct and indirect competition. In a very dynamic environment new competitors may emerge from non-traditional areas. Narrowly focused competitive analysis can lead to an organisation being caught unawares.

All organisations comprise processes that cut across the organisation structure. An organisation should design the process first and then the structure to support it. Generally processes fall into one of two categories, delivery processes or support processes. Delivery processes convert the customers' requirements into the products/services which fulfil these requirements. Support processes exist to ensure that the delivery processes are directed and supported. Typical support processes include strategic planning, recruitment, development of resources etc. Both delivery and support processes can be benchmarked.

With the development of National and International Award Frameworks there has emerged the possibility of benchmarking whole organisations. Often this is done through self-assessment and collaborative benchmarking. Using the European/UK Quality Award Business Excellence Model organisations can assess their own progress and compare themselves to very different types of organisation in order to gain ideas for improvement.

Tree Diagram

Tree Diagrams reveal structure and interrelationships and thus assist in learning and communication. They are used to break down subjects into component parts, projects into tasks and symptoms into root causes. There are three common variants.

The 'Why Why' tree diagram is a cause and effect tool. A symptom is broken down into root causes. At each stage the question 'why' is asked. This is continued until root causes are exposed.

The 'How How' tree diagram is a planning tool. A project or major task is broken down into smaller tasks that can be scheduled. At each stage the question 'how' is asked. This is continued until manageable tasks are identified.

The 'What What' tree diagram is a structuring tool. Products, services, processes, objectives, customer wants and needs, etc. can be broken down into their elements.

At each stage the question 'what does this comprise' is asked. This is continued until enough detail is achieved.

Tree diagrams can go from left to right or vice versa or from top to bottom or vice versa. Because people read from left to right and because most documents are portrait rather than landscape in layout, left to right tree diagrams are often used. An example of a Tree Diagram is shown in Figure 16.

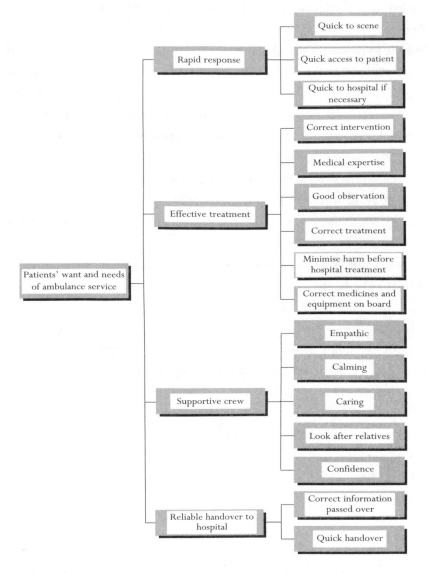

Figure 16. Example of Tree Diagram – Patients' wants and needs of Ambulance Service

Tools for Mapping Processes

Process Definition

The Process Definition is one the most important core tools. It is used to understand existing processes and to design new or improved processes. It ensures that processes are properly scoped and that customers' wants and needs are understood. It also assists in defining other influences on the process and thus helps the team manage complexity.

The shift to process thinking is one of the most profound changes in recent times. Traditional models of organisations concentrated on function, hierarchy and structure. These did not clearly show how work was carried out. With the introduction of the concepts of process, all staff were encouraged to think about their individual customers, both internal and external. People started to concentrate upon the many complex processes that cut across the functions in customer/supplier chains. This improved communications, reduced departmental barriers and led to more effective operations.

Any activity, or series of activities, no matter how large, can be considered as a process. Processes can be broken down into structures of sub-processes. This is called process modelling.

To drive continual improvement the process, not just the outputs, has to be managed. People should be accountable for whole processes wherever possible. Their processes need to be defined and understood. No person is an island and interdependencies need to be clear. People need to know why a process works just as much as why it doesn't. There is no substitute for knowledge.

Because variation exists throughout processes the goal of operators is to get the output 'on target with minimum variation'. There are two types of causes of variation. Special causes are due to assignable factors that are irregular, unstable and hence unpredictable. They must be removed to ensure that the process is stable. Common causes, those variations that are always present, need to be identified and structured improvement applied to reduce process variation. An example of a Process Definition is shown in Figure 17.

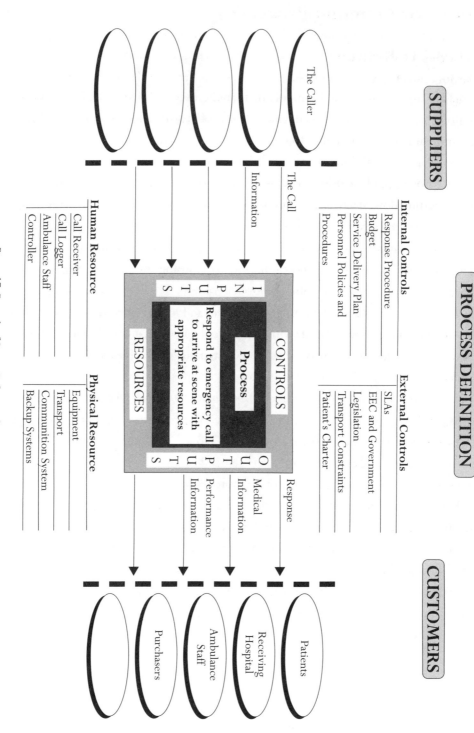

Figure 17. Example of Process Definition for Emergency Call

Flowchart

Flowcharts are used to show the sequence of steps, key decision points, alternative paths and feedback within a process. Flowcharting is a simple way of modelling an existing, new or revised process.

There are many detailed symbols that can be used in flowcharts. Fortunately 80% of flowcharts can be produced with 20% of the available symbols. The five most common are shown in Figure 18.

There are several different types of flowchart. The simple flowchart only uses stop /start, process and decision symbols i.e., the first three symbols in the chart. An input/output flowchart shows how key documents are received and passed on. The inputs and outputs will match those of the process definition. Inputs are shown on the left of the flowchart and output on the right. It may also show data being stored and hence uses all of the five symbols above. Data storage may be within a computer database, a filing cabinet or even a records book.

The deployment flowchart is designed to show which stakeholders are involved in the various steps of the flowchart. The page is divided up into columns, one for each stakeholder. If an activity or decision involves a stakeholder it is drawn within their column. In this way the deployment flowchart winds its way down the page. If more than one stakeholder is involved the symbol is drawn across the necessary columns.

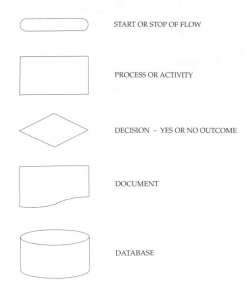

START OR STOP OF FLOW

PROCESS OR ACTIVITY

DECISION – YES OR NO OUTCOME

DOCUMENT

DATABASE

Figure 18. Flowchart symbols

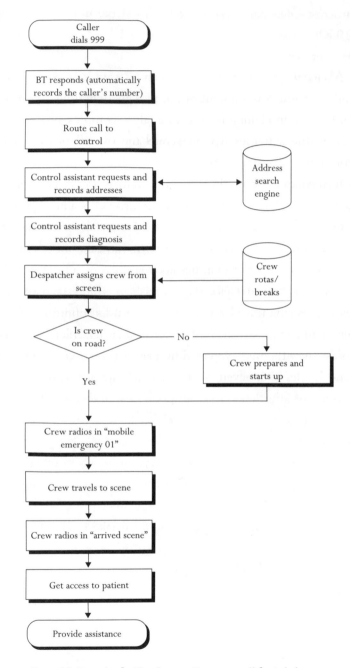

Figure 19. Example of a Flowchart — Emergency call for Ambulance

Feedback is allowed in flowcharts. The result of a decision may be to return to a previous process. A feedback arrow shows this. An example of a Flowchart is shown in Figure 19.

Process Model

Process modelling is a development of the process definition. The two tools are fully compatible. Process modelling is used to analyse complex processes by highlighting and structuring the activities that make up the overall process defined using the process definition.

Process techniques are central to the improvement cycle. Process modelling can be quite specialist but facilitators should know the principles and some of the basic skills. There are many tools and methodologies for modelling processes, including simple flowcharts, deployment flowcharts and SSADM (Structured Systems Analysis Design Methodology). The process model in this book is based on a technique developed by the United States Air Force called IDef0. Many years of application, and a Master of Philosophy research degree, has led the author to conclude that IDef0 offers the maximum usefulness with the minimum complexity particularly for quality-related applications.

The Process definition is completed first so that the boundaries are clear, with the customer and supplier requirements defined and agreed. The definition can then be drawn as a series of interdependent sub-processes. In this way a complex process can be broken down in a structured way. Each of the sub-processes can again be broken down to the next level highlighting what they comprise. This can continue as long as it is valuable. At a certain point flowcharts or work instructions may be more informative. In this way large, complex processes are broken down into manageable elements without losing understanding of the whole.

Research has shown that a typical person can take in about five or six blocks of information at one time from these kinds of diagram and retain an understanding of the linkages. This is why, ideally, there should be no more than five or six sub-processes on any one diagram.

Process models use a numbering system that enables every process to be uniquely identified in the overall model. A sub-process inherits the full number of its 'parent' diagram plus its own number from the page on which it appears. An example of a Process Model can be seen in Figure 9.

Tools for Measuring

Checksheet

Checksheets are used to record the number of incidents of certain events, desired or not, for any process over a specified period of time at a specified time frequency. The information collected using checksheets can then be analysed in more detail.

A checksheet is a data collection form on which it is possible to enter the data by means of a simple check mark. To make totalling easier the five-bar gate system can be used. Four checks are drawn vertically. The fifth is drawn diagonally, creating the appearance of a five bar gate.

Histogram

Histograms show the degree and the nature of variation within an output of a process. Variation occurs and spreads throughout all processes. The nature of the variation needs to be understood. It is useful to represent it graphically using a histogram.

Histograms are barcharts that show the number of occurrences within certain ranges. The distribution's shape and spread can then be analysed.

Run Chart

Run charts are used to show the performance of processes over time. They help identify improvement opportunities as well as providing evidence that improvements have been successful. Measures should be selected that reflect customer satisfaction and other critical success factors.

The subject of measurement is particularly controversial. It needs to be approached with a solid understanding of certain principles. Naive and manipulative measurement is causing a lot of damage throughout the private and public sectors.

Control Chart

Statistical Process Control (SPC) is a tool that identifies whether a process is stable or not and helps people distinguish between special and common causes of variation. Once improvement actions have been implemented SPC control charts provide the evidence as to whether they have been successful. The purpose is to ensure that the process is on target with minimum variation.

Statistical Process Control is a sophisticated tool. It is impossible to do it justice in a summary such as this. There are many good books dedicated to the subject which go into much greater detail (56). However, SPC is too profound a concept to be excluded.

There are two types of variation. Common causes are due to the process itself. They are inherent in the design, implementation and operation of the process. Common cause variation remains the same from day to day. Special causes, however, come from sources outside of the process. They relate to some special event. It is sensible to investigate the actual reason for the variation. It may be operator error, or extreme weather conditions, etc.

The majority of root cause issues come from the system. It is futile exhorting workers to do better. They need to be empowered to improve their own processes. This means training and facilitating them to do the job.

If people cannot distinguish between special and common causes they are likely to take actions which could do a lot of harm. Control charts minimise the risk of mixing up the two situations. The run chart is used to produce the control chart. The control chart has upper and lower control limits. The calculations of the limits vary according to the data and its collection. Expert advice should be sought. Note that the control limits are not the same as the specification limits. The process might be incapable of meeting the specification.

If a point on the control chart lies outside of the control limits then this is likely to be a special cause. Also if three or four consecutive points lie nearer to one of the limits than the mean then this too is likely to be evidence of a special cause. Other variation will come from common causes. This will remain the same unless the system is changed. If consecutive points continue to be nearer to or outside the limits this may be evidence that the system has changed.

Many Western managers treat every signal as if it were special. They do not realise that signals will always vary. The question is what does it tell us. Reacting to every signal can actually increase variation reducing the performance of the process. These managers also tend to blame and reward individuals for common cause variation.

The media is very talented at taking special causes and making them appear to be common. The ensuing public outcry often forces politicians to change legislation and hence change the system. This can also result in poorer quality and wasted resources.

An example of a Control Chart can be seen in Figure 20.

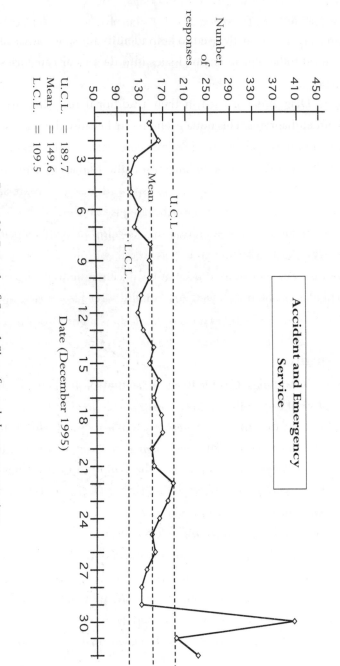

Figure 20. Example of Control Chart for ambulance response times

Tools for Distinguishing Causes from Effects

Fishbone Diagram

Fishbone Diagrams are traditionally used to help identify possible causes of problems. They can also be used to help group many issues into themes or categories relating to a particular subject.

When Fishbone Diagrams are used in their traditional role they are sometimes called cause and effect diagrams. This not a useful name because there are several other cause and effect techniques such as Tree Diagrams and Relation Diagrams.

One particular form of the Fishbone Diagram is the Ishikawa Diagram. This has a generic set of 'bone' labels – Men, Machines, Methods and Materials. This is particularly useful in manufacturing but of little use elsewhere.

In time a non-manufacturing organisation may develop its own generic set. In the meantime the labelling of the bones can be left to the end of the process. In this way the Fishbone Diagram can also be used as an affinity technique to group causes/issues relating to a particular problem/subject. An example of a Fishbone Diagram can be seen in Figure 21.

Relation Diagram

The purpose of the Relation Diagram is to show complex cause and effect chains and to identify root causes or key issues.

Cause and effect relationships are rarely straightforward. In a process the components will tend to interrelate in very dynamic and complex ways. Root causes are often miles way in distance and time from the symptom being investigated. The origins of a problem or issue are often much further 'upstream' in the process or they occurred a long time before the problem was observed.

Fishbone Diagrams and Tree Diagrams are not designed to show very complex relationships. The Relation Diagram can show this detail but this increase in accuracy is often at the expense of simplicity and speed. Relation Diagrams can be difficult to draw and read and take longer than the other cause and effect techniques to produce.

In a Relation Diagram arrows show cause and effect links. An arrow is shown coming from a cause to an effect. A root cause is a cause that only leads to effects and is not caused by anything else on the diagram. Arrows only come out of root causes.

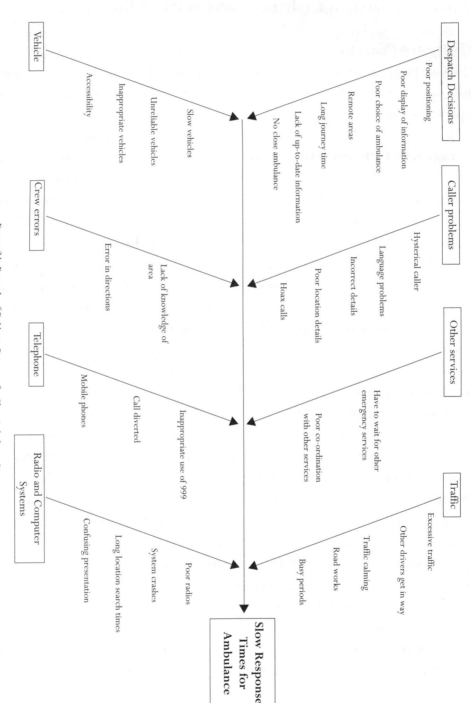

Figure 21. Example of Fishbone Diagram for Slow Ambulance Responses

Sometimes root causes are not identified. This is because circular relationships can occur, such as vicious circles. For example, A causes B, B causes C and C causes A. In these cases the team has to decide where to intervene. This is done by comparing the number of arrows out against the number of arrows in for each issue. Key issues have the largest difference. That is they cause many more issues than other issues cause them. An example of a Relation Diagram can be seen in Figure 32.

Tools for Prioritising and Achieving Consensus

Code of Co-operation

A code of co-operation is established by a group of people. It defines the ideal way in which they want to work and the principles that underpin this way of working. Issues such as building trust, listening, respect, confidentiality, equality, etc., tend to get raised by most groups. This list can be structured and becomes the team's guidelines. If the code is subsequently breached, as it will be at some point, the facilitator has a much stronger mandate to enforce it because the team generated it. Having the code to hand is important and a quick reminder often deals with many potential problems. Humour can be powerful in making a point quickly if someone is breaching the code.

Pareto Principle

The Pareto Principle is used for prioritising. It helps identify the critical few issues on which to focus limited quality improvement resources. The Pareto principle is often referred to as the 80/20 rule. The results of the Pareto analysis are often called the critical few.

In any situation a limited number of issues is likely to have most impact. In problem solving 20% of the root causes account for 80% of the symptom. Pareto is often used in time management where 20% of an individual's time is used to create 80% of their results. There are many examples in all organisations. Twenty percent of a dentist's patients require 80% of the dental work. Twenty percent of customers generate 80% of revenue. Eighty percent of work is done by 20% of suppliers.

Paired Comparison

Paired Comparison is a qualitative technique for prioritising a shortlist of options or issues. It helps achieve consensus through individual voting. This technique is very powerful for removing conflict and bridging differences of opinion because it highlights the degree of consensus within a group.

Paired Comparison works by getting each individual to compare every item with every other, in a pair, and to select which is a greater priority. In quality improvement it is often used to prioritise root cause issues or possible solutions.

Root Cause	Score	Rank	Variance
Poor evaluation	6	7	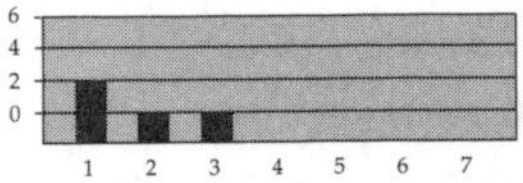
Lack of training	23	4	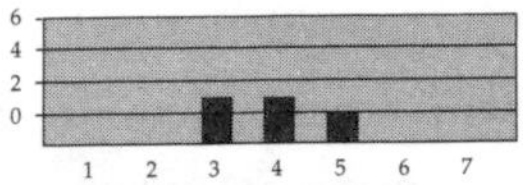
Lack of a clear process	41	1	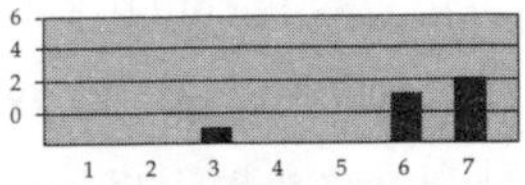
Lack of leadership – style and comfort	30	3	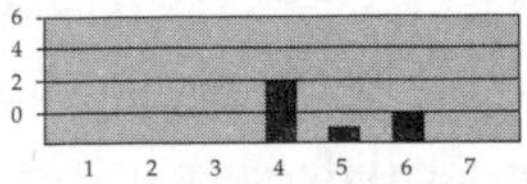
Poor information and communication	20	5	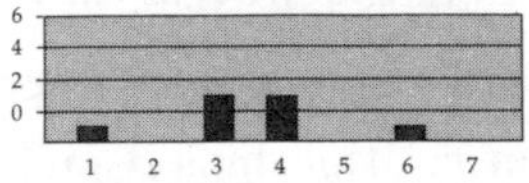
Lack of intregration with strategy, incl. prioritisation	35	2	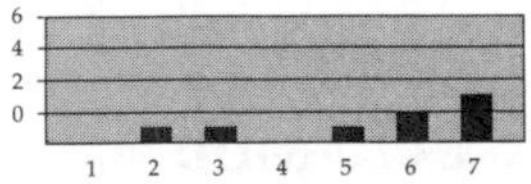
Poor mentoring	13	6	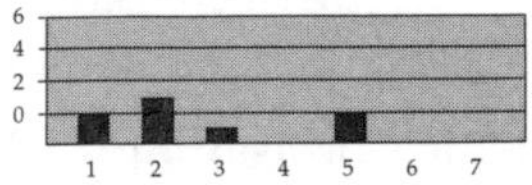

Figure 22. Example of the results of Paired Comparison exploring why Quality Circles are not as effective as they should be.

It should only be used in the absence of hard data. It is subjective, being based on the views and experiences of the people taking part. The results have to be treated cautiously. If the facilitator suspects that 'group think' is occurring other means will have to be found to challenge the team. An example of Paired Comparison is shown in Figure 22.

Matrix

This simple two-dimensional matrix, or table, is designed to show how processes deliver results, such as critical success factors (CSFs). These processes can then be prioritised in order of their actual or potential impact. It enables 'the critical few' processes to be identified.

The CSF/Process Matrix is one example of a two-dimensional matrix. These matrices have outcomes — the 'whats', along the top and the activities, the 'hows', down the left-hand side. A matrix enables complex inter-relationships to be shown. One activity can impact many outcomes, just as one outcome can be influenced by many activities. This is called a 'many to many' relationship and matrices show these actions and reactions most clearly.

In the CSF/Process matrix the outcomes are critical success factors and the activities are processes. Each process's effect on the CSFs can be judged. There are three different judgements: how the process currently performs, how the process could perform if improved or the difference between potential and current performance.

The effect of the process can be classified as strong, medium or weak. If there is no relationship leave a blank. Strong relationships are indicated by a filled in circle with a "3", medium relationships by a "2" and weak relationships by a "1". An example of a Matrix is shown in Figure 23.

Weighted Selection

Weighted Selection is a technique that assists individuals and teams in selecting between a number of options, such as possible improvement actions.

Weighted Selection is more rigorous than paired comparison because options are judged against many factors rather than as a whole against a single criterion. However, it is qualitative and only as good as the judgements that are made. If done carefully with a team it can provide valuable assistance in decision making. An example of Weighted Selection is shown in Figure 24.

PROCESSES \ CSFs	1 Effective people	2 Building customer partnerships	3 Building supplier partnerships	4 Satisfying performance requirements	5 Profile and image	6 Market share	7 Customer satisfaction	8 Financial performance	9	10
Design and build procurement	2	3	3	3	3	3	3	3		
Building	3	3	3	3	3	1	3	2		
Communications	3	3	3	3	3	1	1	3		
Conventional procurement	2	3	3	1	2	3	3	3		
Human Resource management	3	3	3	1	1		1	3		
Business planning	3	3	3		1	3	3	3		
Buying	2		3	3	1	1	3	3		
Customer care	1	3		3	3	1	3	2		

Legend:

3 Strong
2 Medium
1 Weak

Figure 23. Example of CSF/Process Matrix for a construction company

FACTORS / OPTIONS	Purchase price	Drivability	Economy	Safety	Image	Depreciation	TOTALS Weighted Scores	RANK
Weights	2	8	4	4	10	8		
Saab	8 / 16	8 / 64	4 / 16	10 / 40	8 / 80	6 / 48	264	2
Volvo	6 / 12	6 / 48	4 / 16	10 / 40	2 / 20	8 / 64	200	4
BMW	4 / 8	10 / 80	4 / 16	8 / 32	2 / 20	8 / 64	220	3
Mercedes	2 / 4	8 / 64	4 / 16	8 / 32	10 / 100	8 / 64	280	1
Rover	10 / 20	4 / 32	6 / 24	8 / 24	2 / 20	4 / 32	152	5

Figure 24. Example of Weighted Selection — in choosing a new car (Note: this example represents the author's personal opinions)

153

Tools for Encouraging Creativity

Brainstorm

Brainstorming is a divergent technique designed to generate large quantities of ideas from a group of people. It is often used in identifying possible causes of an effect or possible solutions. It encourages creative thinking in an unthreatening environment.

Experiments have shown that brainstorming will typically generate three times the quantity of ideas than that generated by the same individuals working separately. In a good brainstorm team members feed each other ideas and the results are often hybrids of many contributions.

There are several methods of brainstorming each with different strengths and weaknesses. They are all underpinned by some common principles:

People must feel safe to participate.

- No judgement or criticism is allowed during the brainstorm.
- People should strive to generate as many ideas as possible.
- People should be encouraged to be as creative as possible.
- People should be encouraged to build on each other's ideas.
- Person recording writes down exactly what is said.

Formal brainstorming involves going around the group recording one idea at a time. If someone does not have an idea he or she says 'pass' and the brainstorm moves on. The benefits are that everyone gets an equal chance to contribute. However it can be slow, it lacks spontaneity and some people may find it stressful. Formal methods do not work well with groups of more than 12 people.

Informal brainstorming comprises shouting out ideas as soon as they come to mind. It may require several people recording because it can be very rapid. The main benefit is that it is very spontaneous but the more outspoken may dominate and good ideas may be lost. Also there may be very little listening and so ideas are unlikely to be developed.

Silent methods are sometimes used in which each individual records their own ideas. This may ensure greater involvement but increases duplication and does not allow for the development of ideas.

Choice of method will depend on:

- the size of the group.
- whether the group is an effective team or not.
- social and cultural issues.

Once a brainstorm is complete time should be allowed to discuss and analyse what has been generated. Using techniques such as Tree Diagrams or Fishbone Diagrams enables this to be done whilst maintaining momentum.

Mind Map

Mind Maps enable individuals and teams to associate and link ideas relating to a particular theme. This helps to capture, clarify, structure and recall thoughts and concepts. Mind Maps are particularly useful for encouraging creative and divergent thinking. They are also very useful for writing reports and as prompts for presentations, ensuring cohesion and structure.

Tony Buzan has developed mind mapping into a rigorous methodology for learning (57). It is based on a sound understanding of how our minds appear to work. A popular theory distinguishes between the functions of the left and right sides of the brain. The left cortex deals with logic, words, lists, structure, etc. The right cortex is more concerned with daydreaming, colour, creativity, rhythm, etc. Individuals do appear to have preferences but some of the most effective people can utilise both sides.

Brainstorming and mind mapping techniques encourage right brain thinking. Many of the other tools are predominantly logical and analytical. Some innovative organisations are now using drama and art to encourage right brain activity, particularly in visioning. An example of a Mind Map is shown in Figure 25.

De Bono's Techniques

Edward de Bono is one of the world's leading experts in lateral thinking. He has developed a whole portfolio of lateral thinking techniques, all of which can be used successfully with stakeholders to challenge their preconceived ideas (58). A common technique is the Six Thinking Hats. This is based on the premise that there are six responses in innovation. Each may be appropriate at certain times and people may have a predominant response. De Bono uses six coloured hats to signify the different attitudes. The white hat signifies neutrality and information giving; the red, feelings and intuition; the black, caution; the yellow, optimism and positive views; green, creativity and new ideas and blue, the overview. Teams that use the Six Thinking Hats will preface their comments with statements such as 'I'm wearing green, couldn't we do x, y and z'. This signals to others the stance that is being taken and can help promote careful thought.

Other De Bono techniques include the creative pause, generating alternatives and the provocation. In the later people use the word 'Po' to indicate that they are deliberately trying to challenge the prevalent train of thought. The word warns people not to be too judgmental and not to close down any potential opportunities. De Bono does warn about the over use of brainstorming and that it can tend to create more of the same. Another approach advocated by Charles Thompson (59) suggests that teams should be aware of 'killer phrases' such as 'we tried that before', 'with due respect' and 'in the real world' and consciously avoid their use. A Code of co-operation agreed by teams when they start to work together will help avoid these situations and create a climate in which creativity can flourish.

Affinity Diagrams

Affinity Diagrams enable groups to organise and categorise their brainstormed ideas. Natural clusters or grouping of ideas emerge. The pure technique starts by people silently writing ideas onto 'Post It' Notes™. They then place these onto a large landscape wipeboard. The people read all the ideas and then, in silence, group them into as many clusters as appropriate. Once the grouping stage is complete the team decides on the names of the clusters. An example of an Affinity Diagram is shown in Figure 26.

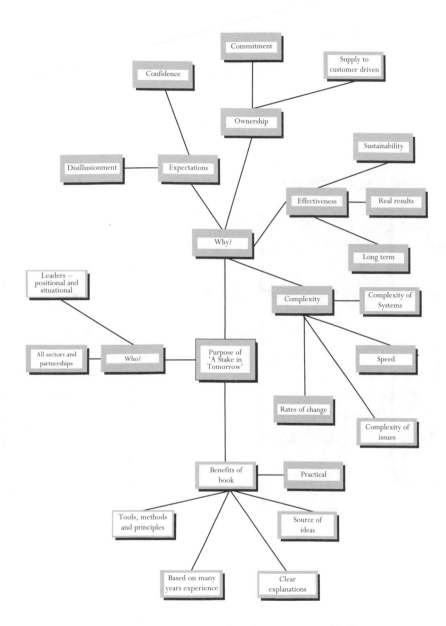

Figure 25. Example of Mind Map – Purpose of this book

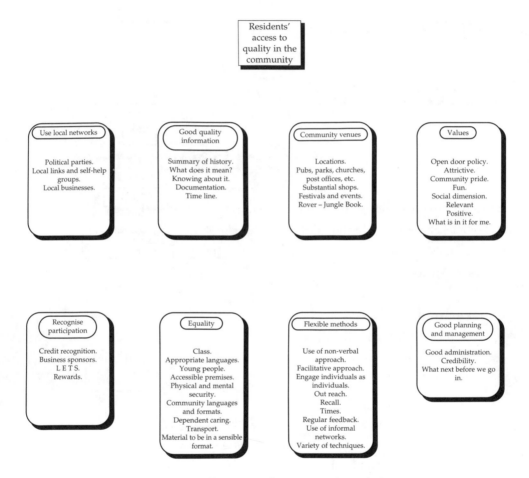

Figure 26. Example of Affinity Diagram for Access to Quality in the Community

Chapter 9

Factors for Successful

Stakeholder Partnerships

This section will explore some of the pre-requisites and other factors for successful stakeholder partnerships. In the third part of the book these factors are used to draw out the practical lessons from applications in private companies, schools, hospitals, charities and whole communities.

Preparedness

Both individual leaders and the organisation as a whole have to be at a certain level of maturity to be able to establish strong partnerships. To attempt to move into this phase of organisational development prematurely will lead to problems, if not failure.

To establish successful partnerships requires a certain type of leadership. This will be explored in more detail later. However, if key leaders in an organisation do not understand the real long-term benefits and are not personally 'grounded' there will be difficulties. The word partnership, like quality, has become a commonly used and somewhat trite term. What does it really mean for the leaders and can they deal with the consequences?

At the heart of the relationship is the concept of mutual benefit or win/win. A sustainable win/win relationship will occasionally require either partner to allow the other to take a gain at their short-term loss. This requires a high degree of personal maturity. It means putting aside rampant competitiveness. It means taking pleasure from others' successes. It means communicating at a deep level and above all it requires a high level of self-confidence.

Transactional Analysis (60) models the personal ego as having three major components – the parent, the adult and the child. For successful negotiation individuals need to communicate at an 'adult to adult' level in the 'here and now'. Unfortunately personal baggage and insecurities may lead to corrupted communication which may undermine relationships and result in poor decisions. Careless communication may trigger a 'critical parent/adapted child' transaction. This is prevalent in manager/staff relationships. Having a very 'hands on' style of management may be very comforting for employees. In fact the last thing many people want is empowerment. A traditional manager/sub-ordinate relationship provides a dangerous 'security blanket'. A paternalistic leader gives staff the chance to disempower themselves. In this situation it is much easier to blame leadership than to take personal responsibility. Many improvement initiatives fail because they assume people want to be empowered and that leaders want to give up power. The very act of a manager inappropriately taking responsibility for an employee's problem may be disempowering and can reinforce the parent/child relationship. To break out of these unproductive relationships requires a great deal of self-awareness, self-reflection and honest communication. What is it in the leader's personality that triggers childlike responses in staff? What is it in the employee's psyche that hears the leader in a critical parent state? Successful partnerships are founded on successful personal relationships. If the potential partners have not reached a high level of self-awareness there will be communication difficulties that could undermine the relationship.

If the leader has to reach a high level of maturity, then so does the organisation as a whole. John Carlisle (61) has developed a model that maps the likely type of relationship to the phase of an organisation's development. At the launch stage the organisation goes through an exciting phase of clear leadership, high flexibility, close involvement and a great deal of informality and initiative. As the organisation grows rapidly it is likely to experience its first crisis. It loses touch with customers and staff. It is likely to respond by moving into the efficient stage. Procedures are introduced and scientific management applied. This often results in the next crisis, a bureaucracy backlash. People feel alienated by the systems. They become 'cogs' in the 'machine'. The third and final stage according to Carlisle is the integrated phase. Managers start to share responsibility with other stakeholders. Systems are liberated and involvement and co-operation grow. These phases are summarised as pioneer, rational and integrated.

Trying to impose a level of stakeholder partnership at an inappropriate phase of development can lead to tensions. In a pioneer phase the organisation has a dominant relationship with its suppliers. This is characterised by persuasion based on personal relationships. During the first crisis the relationship might move to a coercive one based on individual conflicts. If the organisation survives to move into the rational phase, relationships will move to a negotiated position; the supplier becomes a resource. As the organisation moves into the highest level, or integrated phase, the type of relationship changes again. The suppliers tend to become associates and true partners. This is characterised by win/win thinking, joint improvement and development activities and the demise of the traditional customer/supplier boundaries. It is highly probable that throughout this journey the number of suppliers will be reduced dramatically. It is very difficult, if not impossible, to have highly integrated relationships with thousands of suppliers.

The development of ISO9000 as a supplier management tool reinforces the validity of Carlisle's model. As organisations move from the pioneer to the rational phase they often introduce internal quality assurance systems such as ISO9000. This is then passed back through the supply chain. Eighty percent of UK companies that are ISO9000 certified did it because a major customer 'forced' them (62). Most organisations then realise that quality assurance provides a low level of supplier partnership. They then, hopefully, move into the integrated phase based on much broader alliances. Many such as Rover Group and ICL use the EFQM's Business Excellence Model (63) as a framework for joint and self-assessment. The phases of development may explain why many Japanese companies have been loath to adopt ISO9000. They are already in the integrated phase and ISO9000 takes them back to the rational phase. An organisation should understand where it is in the phases of development and choose an appropriate supplier management model.

Moving too quickly may result in the supplier management strategy being ahead of the organisation's maturity. This could result in more rapid development or could create unacceptable tensions. In one TEC the Total Quality Manager wanted to move to meaningful relationships with the Training Providers founded on joint improvement activity and shared training. The organisation was actually moving from the pioneer to the rational phase and the initiative was so far ahead of the organisation's development that mixed messages were sent to the suppliers, resulting in a less than successful outcome. Six years after its foundation the organisation is now ready to return to this supplier management approach.

In summary both people and organisations need to be at a certain level of maturity to implement the kind of stakeholder partnerships advocated in this book.

Critical Success Factors

Ten years experience of implementing stakeholder partnerships throughout all sectors and communities has enabled the author to summarise the factors critical for success. They are as follows.

- Effective Leadership.
- Common Purpose.
- Suitable Skills.
- Continual Improvement.
- Strong Relationships.
- Sustainable Results.
- Sound Evaluation.

Each will now be explored in more detail.

Effective Leadership

Much has already been written in this book on the need for sound leadership. This needs to be summarised, and in some cases, explored in more detail. It is imperative that individual leaders from all the organisations forming a partnership have reached a high level of personal maturity based on self-awareness and self-esteem. Without this the foundations for partnership will be weak.

Leaders need to move from a position of paternalism to stewardship. Peter Block in his book entitled *Stewardship* (64) identifies six underpinning beliefs for leaders to accept.

The first is that people really long to invest their energy in things that matter. Leaders need to find ways of affirming, through actions not just words, that people are truly central to the organisation. People are born with an incredible love of learning and zest for life. Some may even survive the education system to bring this zeal into the workplace. Few will keep it for very long in traditional patriarchies. If you really believe people are central to success how do your actions as a leader reflect this belief?

The second belief is that the old models, or paradigms, of management are no longer working. Partnership is founded on the belief that sharing power and responsibility in a balanced way is the only way to proceed to the new ways of working.

Thirdly we need to let go of the parent/child principle in leadership. People have to be empowered, with clear responsibilities, to create the customer-focused or quality culture.

The fourth principle is that leaders need to re-integrate the management of the work and the doing of the work. Block refers to the two-tier class system that exists in most organisations. This is just as insidious as any class system such as those that still prevail in the UK and India. We need to reduce staff support functions and return them to the line function where they belong.

As Deming said 'the system is unlikely to change itself'. Most change programmes have experienced the problem that the very patriarchy that is driving the change is the very one in need of fundamental review. One can't cure the disease by implementing more of the illness. This is the fifth principle.

The sixth and final principle is that processes and structures need to be redesigned to reflect the former principles. If a leader truly accepts these beliefs then he or she will want to see them present in everything the organisation does. There are few examples of this kind of principle-centred leadership. In the UK Branson of Virgin and Roddick of the Body Shop are in the vanguard.

Block has also summarised nine behaviours that logically flow from these beliefs. They are:

1. Maximise the choice for those closest to the work.
2. Reintegrate the managing and the doing of the work.
3. Let measurements and controls serve the core workers.
4. Yield on consistency across groups and support local solutions.
5. Service is everything.
6. De-glorify management as a job title and de-mystify the staff functions.
7. End secrecy.

8. Demand a promise. Rights and responsibilities go hand in hand (65).

9. Redistribute wealth. Base the compensation process on exceptional service.

Leaders need to change from being patriarchs to stewards or, in the language of quality, they need to change from being controllers to facilitators. We need to break away from traditional views of leaders. Leadership does not just come from position. It also happens informally in certain situations. The employee who takes exceptional action to resolve a customer complaint is showing situational leadership. Most people have leadership roles outside of work. Recognise this latent potential. Leadership is not about the size of your 'empire'. Some of the world's most influential leaders, such as Martin Luther King and Gandhi, had few or no direct reports. Organisations need to find ways to develop informal as well as formal leadership.

Maybe the most important principle is to lead by example. Rover Group directors spend time on the 'tracks' building cars. ICL's directors spend time staffing the Help Desks. If you say that customers are important allocate time to spend with them.

On the subject of time, few leaders allocate enough to allow for transformation. 3M, a pioneer in innovation and continual improvement, allocate between five percent and ten percent of everyone's time for improvement activities. Every person should be responsible for operating their processes, improving them and helping others improve theirs. Change takes time, usually much more than originally forecast. One of the most often stated frustrations from staff is that time is not allocated for self-development and improvement.

A strong partnership can only be achieved if leaders recognise and respect differences of world view. Public/private sector partnerships are notoriously difficult to manage. One of the reasons is that the different sectors come from fundamentally different philosophies. A teacher is unlikely to accept that they are in education to make their school a business. Equally business leaders cannot afford to be too altruistic.

Common Purpose

'Without vision, the people perish' is a wise quote from the Bible. A sense of shared purpose is critical for success. This does not come from remote words written into a strategic document. People have their own purposes and visions and these need to align to the partnership's collective ones. A sense of constancy and consistency of purpose can only be achieved over a long period of time through stakeholder involvement. Words are not enough. The purpose needs to be lived out on a day-to-day basis and stakeholders need to be able to relate their work to the achievement of the long-term goals.

Any statement of purpose must be driven by the wants and needs of the beneficiaries, or customers, of the work. The best way to understand each other's short and long-term wants and needs is to build strong personal relationships. Visions can be lost and processes need to be in place to reaffirm and check direction.

Suitable Skills

Involvement in stakeholder partnerships involves different skills and attributes for all participants. Processes need to be in place for ongoing self-development and training. Both confidence and competence need to be enhanced. There are many hard and soft skills that people will need to participate effectively in partnerships.

People will need to be grounded in the analytical techniques of process improvement. They will need to be able to understand complex systems and interactions. They will also need to understand the dangers and limitations of measurement.

On the softer side they will need to create environments in which innovation can flourish. They will need an understanding of practical psychology. What makes people 'tick'? How can one build on people's inherent differences? How does one minimise and manage conflict? How do you put yourself in someone else's shoes? The Native Americans having a saying that if you really want to understand someone 'walk a hundred miles in their moccasins'. Stakeholders have to understand how to build each other's confidence. One does not do this by fear and blame.

A useful exercise at the start of any partnership work is to do a simple skills audit. Ask the people to list their skills, attributes and experiences that may have a bearing on the task. The results are usually astonishing and help to build respect and well as identifying invaluable expertise.

Finally the partnership will require a number of people trained specifically to facilitate processes such as strategic planning and improvement. These people will need to be competent and confident to facilitate teams of very diverse stakeholders. Usually these people come from all strata of the organisation. They will need to be good communicators and listeners. They will also have to have empathy for people and a great deal of tenacity. A good facilitator guides the process and does not influence the outcome. At the end of the task the participants will probably say that they did it themselves.

Skills should be developed continuously. A core of skills will be required to commence the work and to deal with the 'minefields' that lie ahead. Don't under-invest in training and development. The cost of ignorance is very high.

Continual Improvement

Continual improvement needs to apply to every aspect of the stakeholder partnership. If it doesn't, what is the point of having the partnership? Any approach to continual improvement needs to be founded on distinguishing special and common causes, filtering the root causes from the symptoms and leaving no stone unturned.

It is important to follow a structured, disciplined approach. A range of tools and techniques will need to be used when appropriate. Tools and techniques need to be modified to take into account cultural and intellectual differences.

It is sometimes difficult to temper enthusiasm. Improvement is about doing the right things right. People who are in hurry often jump straight into improvement without properly defining and analysing the situation. Watch out for the manic or the macho ones.

If stakeholder teams are correctly formed they will be able to involve themselves in joint improvement, including problem solving, as well as developing whole new opportunities. Teams need to keep striving for improvement based on sound learning. Continual improvement is built on continual learning. Someone who doesn't understand the past is destined to keep making the same mistakes.

Strong Relationships

Relationship founded on trust is at the heart of partnership. We all know from bitter experience that trust takes years to build and it can be destroyed in minutes. Trust is an example of one of the many important 'unknowns and unknowables' in management. We know when it is present but we can't put a hard and fast measure on it.

To start to build trust someone has to put down his or her 'weapons' first. This is a very unnatural thing to do. The late Larrae Rocheleau, former Superintendent of

Mount Edgecumbe High School, used to insist, metaphorically, that all 'weapons' were left behind for good. Remember that the majority of root causes come from the system not the person, so why do we need weapons? There is a wonderful summary of one of the key differences between Japanese and American cultures in the movie *The Rising Sun*. One of the Japanese executives explains to Wesley Snipes that Americans are obsessed with fixing the blame whereas the Japanese concentrate on fixing the problem. They actually go further than this by working to prevent problems occurring in the first place.

Many of the more macho readers of this book, if there are any left, will not like the next revelation. Harvey Stewart, who has spent many years of his life working with disadvantaged groups, calmly declares that love is the foundation for meeting the needs of others in order to accomplish good. He articulates a virtuous circle whereby quality time builds knowledge, knowledge builds trust and trust builds love. Love creates the desire to spend more quality time together and so on.

On a more practical note, declaring and documenting the underpinning ethics or code of a partnership can do much to build strong relationships. Be careful of nice sounding, politically correct platitudes. Only put down in writing what you really mean. Otherwise you will create a 'rod for your own back'.

The need to understand world views has already been discussed. It is important to respect the right of people to hold different views and resist the temptation to try to change them. You may not agree with others' views but you need to respect their right to have them. To truly understand different perspectives means spending time in others' environments. The growth in international trade has highlighted the inability of people to communicate across cultures. Many amusing examples have been documented when Western cultures meet Eastern ones. But even within nations these differences exist. To try to understand diversity it is sometimes useful to find out how a culture measures success. In Native American cultures your stature in the community is linked to family. Family comes first and anyone trying to encourage enterprise in these communities would do well to recognise this. Once cultures have been understood it is imperative to avoid manipulating their system to get your desired result. This will only serve to undermine that valuable commodity – trust. Respecting cultural diversity is not about maintaining the status quo but making sure that one is 'slow to be fast'.

In the end a partnership can only be sustained if there is a genuine need for one another. It also means that any partner has the right to say 'no deal' if mutual benefit cannot be found. Never enter into win/lose relationships. They will always end up as lose/lose ones in the long-term.

Some of the key words for successful stakeholder partnerships are freedom, trust, sensitivity and vulnerability. Think of any successful personal relationship and it is likely that you will find the same attributes. After all, an organisational partnership is the sum of many personal ones. The condition of strong relationships cannot be created quickly. They have to be nurtured and developed and will obviously suffer setbacks. If these are recognised quickly and honestly, the relationships can be repaired.

Sustainable Results

Without results the relationship cannot be mutually beneficial. Avoid the natural desire to achieve a lot quickly. Growth in partnerships is often exponential, with little appearing to happen in the early days and then rapid results later on. It is important to manage all stakeholders' expectations carefully in the early days. Funders of these partnerships are particularly prone to demanding too much too soon. Output-related funding, if it does not respect the gestation times involved, can destroy what would otherwise be successful projects. One does not keep digging the seed up to see how it is growing.

In practice it may not be possible to secure the time needed for longer-term results. It may be important for funders and morale to show some early results. In these cases select 'the low fruit for picking'. Target some issues that may be easy to resolve and will achieve a lot of stakeholder goodwill. Be careful of appearing manipulative if you have to do this.

Sustainability is an issue which needs to be considered if the partnership is only going to exist for a predefined period. Exit strategies should form part of the initial planning. How is the partnership going to ensure that its work is sustained and develops after its demise?

Sound Evaluation

Sound evaluation is the means to demonstrate that sustainable results are being achieved. Evaluation must be designed into the processes at the start. It should be carried out systematically and regularly. There are many evaluation tools varying from 'happy sheets' to full scale external evaluations. Get all stakeholders into the practice of reviewing everything they do. When time is short evaluation is often one of the first things to be left out.

If a meeting of stakeholders is to be held make sure that the aims are clearly stated at the start. Do the work and then spend some time reviewing. The choice of review mechanism will depend on accuracy required, external credibility, cost and time. In the example of a working session it might be quite adequate to take five or ten minutes to review the strengths of the work, including the way in which it was done, and the areas needing improvement.

In some cases there may already exist formal evaluation mechanisms. Many of these can contravene the principles of effective partnership working. The Office of Standards in Education in the UK uses a very rigorous and costly model of evaluation. Success depends, to some degree, on the luck of the draw. A good lead inspector will work in partnership with a school to drive out fear and achieve a real desire to improve. Less enlightened ones can create all sorts of game playing. If a stakeholder partnership exists to improve the quality of education in a community it may make sense to use elements of the OFSTED model to review progress.

There is a growing trend, both in the US and Europe, to use National Quality Award Frameworks for self-assessment. This is encouraging because it puts the onus back on the organisations to carry out their own assessment of progress. The British Quality Foundation, responsible for promoting and managing the UK Quality Award, has developed a process called Validscore which provides a degree of external validation to self-assessment if this is required.

Part 3

Examples of Stakeholding

Chapter 10

Stakeholding in the Private Sector

The examples are drawn from what is traditionally regarded as the private sector. The distinction between private and public is rapidly becoming obsolete, with many ex-public sector organisations entering the 'twilight zone' of government agencies and quangos. The examples are not just selected to highlight what has worked but also what has not. The examples are structured around the critical success factors for successful stakeholder partnerships. As John Dewy said in 1906 'A model is not something to be replicated but rather it is a demonstration of the feasibility of a principle with an explanation, the roadblocks encountered and how they were resolved'. Hopefully this part of the book will provide valuable information, but be wary of copying.

The Private Sector as a System

Having stressed the importance of systems thinking it is appropriate to start each of the chapters in this part of the book with an overview of the total system into which the organisations fit (Figure 27).

Private sector organisations supply products and services in complex customer/supplier chains. They are strongly influenced by national and international legislation as well as guidelines of best practice. At the end of any supply chain will be the end user. Companies focus on the implications of their products throughout their useful lives and many are starting to concentrate on disposal and recycling. The nature of guidance and control of firms will depend on their constitutions and type of ownership but obviously the shareholders have great influence to bear on the performance of the system.

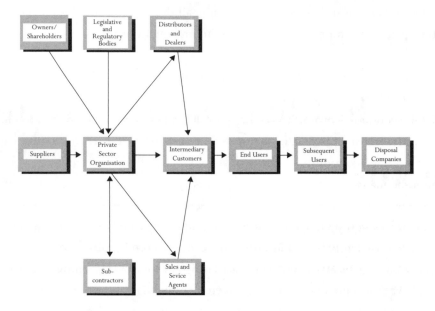

Figure 27. Private Sector as a System

Background Information

The examples are drawn from a range of companies including an international IT systems and services company, currently largely owned by a Japanese electronics firm, a medium-sized construction company, a long established, family-owned waste management firm, a world-class hotel and a world-renowned retailer.

International Computers Ltd (ICL) started its quality journey in 1985. Divisions of the company have won the European Quality Award once and the UK Quality Award twice. ICL is recognised as a world leader recovering from near liquidation in the early Eighties. In the UK the company most often associated with quality is the retailer Marks & Spencer. Its approach to supplier partnerships is acknowledged as being one of the best. Hemmings Waste Management is a family-owned business that is in the process of growing rapidly by applying the principles of stakeholding. It is demonstrating that the principles are applicable to small businesses. The Royal Crescent Hotel in Bath is one of the country's best hotels placed in the prestigious Crescent. Pearce Group PLC has been implementing some very innovative programmes to break down the barriers that often exist between professionals in this very traditional industry sector. The one thing all these companies have in common is a determination to improve to ensure maximum benefit for all their stakeholders.

Stakeholding in the Private Sector – Effective Leadership

Sadly this section has proven to be the most difficult to complete. There are plenty of examples of unprincipled leadership in the private sector. Nearly all industry leaders say that they are committed to their stakeholders but the requirements, often short-term, of the management and the shareholders often dominate to the detriment of the others. Consider again the actual case of a reputable, hi-tech manufacturer that was committed to investing in its people and then proceeded to sack its apprentices and ask its staff for a pay freeze whilst awarding the directors pay increases of up to 50%. The difference between rhetoric and action is transparent to other stakeholders, particularly the staff. What incentive is there to improve if only one stakeholder group benefits?

When people are asked to identify examples of good leadership they often come up with a similar shortlist. Head of the list is Richard Branson of Virgin. Branson seems to instil a tremendous amount of loyalty in his staff by selecting them carefully and then truly empowering them. Another popular person is Anita Roddick of the Body Shop. Her company was founded on strong ethical principles and whilst recently they have been criticised there is no doubt that she tries to practise what she preaches. Other quality leaders often mentioned are Peter Bonfield, former Chief Executive of ICL, and John Towers, former Chief Executive of Rover Group. It is impossible to be prescriptive as to what makes a good leader but the former all have clear visions, empower people, do what they say and are not afraid to make tough decisions.

ICL's leaders have shown incredible tenacity under Bonfield's overall leadership. The quality journey, started in 1985, has been sustained and developed to date. The best examples come from D2D, which became so successful that it now operates as an independent company. ICL Manufacturing used to be the epitome of everything that was wrong in British industry. There had been under-investment in both plant and people, industrial relations were based on conflict and the product had a poor reputation. The revolution started with the senior managers themselves. All of them went through extensive retraining and shared responsibility for the transformation. One of the best ways to learn is to teach others and the senior managers were responsible for delivering training to their own staff. Many union leaders became trainers and facilitators themselves. This approach showed, by action not just words, that the majority of leaders were serious about improvement.

Once the culture was established with staff, senior managers took their message to other stakeholders including suppliers, customers and even the local community. ICL has pioneered joint working with local schools and other businesses. Alastair Kelly, Managing Director of D2D, is also an active leader of Staffordshire Training and Enterprise Council, helping to support local business. ICL managers regularly appear on the conference circuits around the world promoting this way of working.

Even after the start of the transformation ICL has had to contend with difficult business situations. Their distinguishing trait has been their determination to proceed. During the troughs new approaches have been introduced to build on the culture already established. Whilst others have given up, ICL has moved on to more profound implementations of the principles of stakeholding. Some of their actions do appear to contravene some principles. D2D is highly dependent on contract staff. It is interesting to see how they have sustained commitment to the company with less than desirable commitment to staff.

Stakeholding in the Private Sector – Common Purpose

In the early Nineties, Pearce Group PLC went through a process to achieve a common purpose. A cross-section of managers and staff were brought together for several days. The team started by identifying all of the company's stakeholders. This list included primary customers, requiring living and working environments, as well as secondary customers such as users of the buildings and the local community and environment. Partners included architects, lawyers and sub-contractors. Other stakeholders included the Health and Safety Executive and council planners.

The stakeholders' wants and needs were identified and potential conflicts highlighted. Key performance indicators were defined to embrace the 'critical few' wants and needs. After reviewing competitor performance and potential future influences the team produced a statement of purpose. 'We at Pearce Construction, in partnership with our suppliers, are committed to exceeding customer expectations in the design, construction and maintenance of living and working environments.' Next the team identified the factors critical for the achievement of this purpose. The company's processes were then mapped against the critical success factors and critical processes highlighted.

The process broke down some of the prevailing paradigms. At the start the purchasing manager was convinced that it was not possible to reduce the number of suppliers in order to create longer-term partnerships. At the end it was agreed to develop a process to do just that.

Stakeholding in the Private Sector – Suitable Skills

Roger Leveson, Personnel Manager at Pearce Group, has been instrumental in creating a unique development programme for construction professionals. New types of procurement, such as design and build, require the contractor to co-ordinate and manage the complete process from initial requirements through to hand-over. Under traditional contracting the external architect represents the client and oversees building works, leaving the contractor's team to deal with the day-to-day co-ordination of the project. Skills required are more technical than interpersonal, task-focused rather than people-centred. Today the professional needs a new set of skills. He or she needs to work within a multi-disciplinary team of diverse professionals, technicians and artisans.

To provide the skills and competencies required by the new generalists a development programme has been delivered to architects, surveyors and site managers. The programme has involved other stakeholders such as customers and sub-contractors. The curriculum concentrates on the softer skills required to co-ordinate the stakeholders throughout the whole process. The initial results are very favourable with trainees applying their new skills on long-term projects. The curriculum covers leadership, stakeholding, strategy, learning and continual improvement as well as the latest concepts of project management. It is intended to offer the programme to external stakeholders in due course.

Stakeholding in the Private Sector – Continual Improvement

There are many examples of successful continual improvement in the private sector. The automotive, electronic and aerospace sectors have been in the vanguard. There are fewer examples from smaller businesses. These two examples are from such organisations.

Hemmings Waste Management started its transformation by implementing Investors in People. The company recognised that they needed to go further to address some of the thornier problems. Both managers and staff had highlighted improving the quality of vehicle maintenance as a priority. The relationships between the maintenance team and the drivers were starting to deteriorate and as a result customer service was being affected.

All the stakeholders were involved in brainstorming key words, which they were able to use as the basis for the final quality objective. This was that on completion of the task the team was to have implemented improvements which would ensure that all vehicles leaving the workshop would be capable of doing the job safely and legally. This would result in less defects, lower downtime, greater driver satisfaction and ultimately increased customer satisfaction. A rough Process Definition had been completed prior to the first meeting in order to identify who should be part of the team. The team comprised mechanics, drivers, operations controllers, sales people and two representatives from senior management. This was the first time such a team of stakeholders had met. A final version of the Process Definition was produced at the first meeting. This included identifying the drivers' and the operational controllers' wants and needs as regards the maintenance process. The main activities within the process were identified and a rough flowchart produced. The team agreed a schedule to complete the improvement cycle. The first meeting lasted one-day, so a considerable amount of work was completed. People at the first session agreed to meet several times over a period of three months.

From the Process Definition several key measures were identified, including number of breakdowns and availability of vehicles. Measurement charts were used to show the performance of the process. The Pareto Principle helped the group identify the breakdown of Trade Waste vehicles as a priority. Further data were gathered and analysed. The team then brainstormed all the possible causes of Trade Waste Vehicle breakdowns. They grouped these using a Fishbone Diagram and showed some of the root causes through the use of a Relation Diagram. The eight root causes were prioritised using Paired Comparison. Driver misuse, due to lack of appropriate training and understanding, was identified as the priority issue.

The team then brainstormed many possible improvements including formal and informal training, job shadowing, better coaching, etc. It was decided to introduce a system which would build closer relationships between individual drivers and the mechanics. This included aspects of shadowing as well as much quicker and more direct ways of providing two-way feedback. The team designed an approach using a simple flowchart and then mapped out the main activities required to implement the new process through the use of a rudimentary critical path analysis. The approach was introduced according to the plan.

The initial feedback is very positive. Final evaluation has included all the stakeholders including the drivers and the fitters. Progress of the team has been communicated throughout the project. Many small businesses believe that such a stakeholder approach is too time-consuming and costly. However, engaging the brainpower of the different stakeholders ensures better solutions, implemented more quickly and effectively.

Another example of continual improvement came from The Royal Crescent Hotel. The new manager, with a track record of improvement and service, called together a team of stakeholders including 'front of house' staff, waiters and even the chef! The Hotel's restaurant is one of the finest in the country for food. However, discussions with American customers highlighted that the service was considered to be too slow. The team identified all the wants and needs of a hotel restaurant experience and set about reducing waiting time. By flowcharting the process and by collecting data the staff were able to make significant improvements for less patient guests very rapidly, hence ensuring that the service matched the quality of the food.

Stakeholding in the Private Sector – Strong Relationships

Marks & Spencer started as a penny stall in the North of England in 1884. It now employs 62,000 people worldwide with 300 stores in the UK alone. *Fortune* magazine ranks it as one of the most successful retailers in the world. The business is built on principles of quality and value, investment in technology, supporting British industry, long-term partnerships with suppliers, sharing success with staff and shareholders, maintaining good relationships with staff, customers and local communities and meeting environmental responsibilities. M&S works in partnership throughout the supply chain with suppliers of raw materials, merchandise, services and systems.

M&S does not manufacture any of its products. However, the strength of its relations with its suppliers means that it is truly a manufacturer without factories. As long ago as the mid-Thirties the company established a textile laboratory, a merchandise development department and a design department. Specialists from these departments work throughout the whole length of the supply chain, setting stringent quality standards. This consistency, particularly in colour control, has enabled M&S to offer flexibility and confidence to customers worldwide. By taking the voice of the customers to the suppliers, all parties have been able to innovate rapidly. The easy-care fabric technologies were developed by M&S and shared with its suppliers. In this way suppliers got access to information and technology that would have been prohibitively expensive. The very survival of the British shirt industry is attributed to M&S.

The commercial benefits for M&S are obvious but the suppliers gain, too. They share in the knowledge of the company's future direction, volumes are easier to forecast, prices are fair and payment is prompt but, most of all, being one of M&S's suppliers gives a great deal of security. One company has been in this fortunate position for over 100 years. M&S takes the view that it would rather support an existing supplier to develop a new product range than risk the uncertainties of buying from an unknown source.

M&S expects its suppliers to adhere to its principles, which includes the welfare of staff. It has been promoting ethical business long before it became fashionable. It will come as no surprise that the key ingredient for success is trust. The relationships are not between organisations but between individuals and there are no short cuts. It has to take time. The model of partnership working pioneered by M&S is very similar to that developed by the Japanese automotive industry in the Fifties. When George Bush negotiated better access for US automotive component manufacturers to the Japanese market, he underestimated the value placed on long-term relationships. These companies are not going to sacrifice all of the commercial benefits on price alone.

Stakeholding in the Private Sector – Sustainable Results

Possibly the best results in the private sector have been achieved by D2D. They started implementing Total Quality, founded on the principles of stakeholding, in 1985. A summary of their achievements follows:

* Return on capital employed up to 11%.
* £120K revenue per employee (best competitor achieves £98K).
* 'Inventory turns' per year up from 3 in 1985 to 9 in 1993.
* Number of major customers doubled in three years.
* Customer scorecards averaged 80%.
* On-time delivery up from 80% to 96%.
* Self-assessment scores based on BEM between 700 and 800 points (won EQA in 1994).
* Higher levels of staff involvement in improvement than Nissan, Milliken and IBM (UK).
* Training days per member of staff almost tripled.
* 'Time to market' best in class on 6 out of 7 categories.
* Cost of non-conformance halved from 1989 to 1994.

Because of D2D's sustained effort customers, staff and suppliers have all benefited in tangible ways. The local community has also benefited in the sharing of resources and skills along with job creation. The environment has also benefited as waste has been reduced and the use of harmful chemicals has diminished.

Stakeholding in the Private Sector – Sound Evaluation

ICL has some of the best expertise in self-assessment. It was one of the first companies in the UK to adopt the Business Excellence Model for evaluating its progress. This involves monitoring the levels of satisfaction of all the stakeholders, including society. In a recent interview with Estelle Clark, ICL Quality Director, the company's future use of self-assessment was revealed. She has concluded that there are two applications. The first is to fully integrate the model into the company's long-term strategy and the second is to to win awards. ICL has demonstrated the first application admirably. Now it is busy integrating the BEM as the core of all strategic planning.

ICL sees its role developing as a strategic convenor for the emerging technologies. It wants to concentrate on how its customers can exploit the rapidly changing world of technology and education, and what this will mean for future communities. It is concentrating on facilitating change in retail, leisure and learning. In the past ICL companies used the BEM to evaluate all aspects of the business. They used to start with leadership and work forward (see Figure 11). This type of evaluation tended to generate enormous lists of non prioritised improvements. Now the most senior managers are using the model to define desired business results such as penetration of new markets and revenue growth and then working back through the nine elements to decide what needs to be improved to achieve the results. This means that the model is now at the heart of strategic and business planning. The strategic agreements are then formulated with the companies, as well as support services. These are then used to monitor progress. The transition may seem subtle but the implications are profound. The stakeholding approach will be fully integrated into all aspects of the businesses. Few companies can claim this achievement.

Chapter 11

Stakeholding in Education

Education as a System

Having stressed the importance of systems thinking it is appropriate to start each of the chapters in this part of the book with an overview of the total system into which the organisations fit (Figure 28).

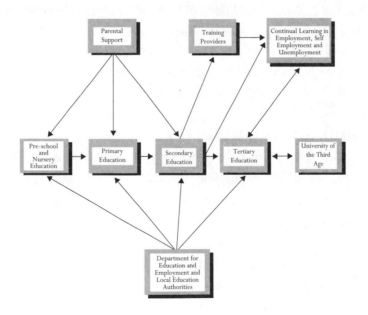

Figure 28. Education as a System

The education system should operate from 'cradle to grave'. Research is showing that the years zero to three are critical for the future success of the child. A supportive parental environment dramatically improves the child's performance in all aspects of development, not just the academic. Apart from a growing minority of parents who are deciding to school their children at home, most parents opt for the State System of Primary and Secondary Education. Growing numbers of young adults are choosing to go on to university. Some opt for new government initiatives such as Modern Apprenticeships via publicly funded Training Providers. At the end of their formal education young people will find themselves employed, self-employed or unemployed. Continual learning opportunities exist for all of these people through a plethora of means. These include full-time courses, government-funded retraining or distance learning programmes. The 'University of the Third Age' is a rapidly expanding group of retired people creating opportunities to continue to develop new skills and knowledge. Education is strongly influenced by both national and local government. The special education system is also becoming far more integrated into the mainstream.

As Charles Handy states 'If changing is really learning, if effective organisations need more and more intelligent people, if careers are shorter and more changeable, above all, if more people need to be self-sufficient for more of their lives, then education has to become the single most important investment that any person can make in their own destiny – education needs to be re-invented' (66).

Background Information

The following examples are drawn for a range of UK and US schools. One large UK comprehensive school has been struggling with the implementation of quality for five years. Another, Smith's Wood School in the Midlands, is applying the principles of stakeholding with all the partner primary schools. Many of the improvement initiatives in UK education are actively being supported by leading private and public sector organisations such as ICL, Land Rover and The Royal Mail. In the US lessons are drawn from Mt Edgecumbe High School, Sitka, Alaska, and a failed New American School Initiative. The school in Alaska is probably the world's leader in applying the principles in this book and has achieved dramatic, sustained improvements. MEHS is a state-operated residential school serving students throughout Alaska. Ages range from 14 to 18. There are approximately 300 students of whom 82% are native Alaskans.

Stakeholding in the Education – Effective Leadership

One of the best examples of principle-centred leadership in education, and possibly in all organisations, is that of the late Larrae Rocheleau, former Superintendent of Mt Edgecumbe School. Larrae did not generate the idea of applying Dr Deming's ideas to a School; it came from the classroom of David Langford and his students. However, Larrae had already made a commitment to actively support innovation. David would have been 'the daisy in the compost heap' without Larrae's support. It would have been easier for the school to remove the daisy rather than move the compost!

Larrae gave David the space and support to prove his ideas. David's students then applied pressure to get other teachers to adopt this radically different way of working. This was truly an example of 'bottom up' transformation, but it had the full support of the most senior teacher. Initially one or two other teachers actively got involved and over a period of eight years almost all the other teachers 'signed up'.

What made Larrae special? Firstly he loved teaching and he loved children. He was a great reader and researcher and always on the lookout for new ideas. He certainly had a great charisma and could make all sorts of people feel valued. He was a great communicator, often using his strong sense of humour to convey complex ideas. But perhaps his greatest strength was that of never being afraid to admit his failings and mistakes. A measure of the man was the response of the community to his untimely death.

Rob Hawkins, Head teacher of Smith's Wood Comprehensive School and Lee Regan, Headteacher of St John the Baptist Primary School, both in Solihull, share many of Larrae's positive attributes. They are both committed educationalists, both relish innovation and can inspire others. Both have realised that they can only achieve long-term improvements for their students by engaging the whole community. Rob has set about improvement by forming a strong partnership founded on shared power and responsibility with all the partner schools in Smith's Wood. Lee has started by concentrating on building the confidence and skills of his students' parents. Both are adopting lateral, systematic and long-term approaches.

In the US the average employment of a Superintendent is just more than two years! Head teachers in the UK tend to stay for longer periods. However, change of leadership presents one of the greatest threats to the stakeholding culture. There is a strong tendency to recruit Head teachers from outside. This can be healthy, but if the new leader is not respectful of the work already done, in extreme cases, it can lead to the demise of this way of working. It is imperative to ensure that the values and principles are built into the recruitment process. Governors need to be fully aware of the existing and desired cultures when selecting future Head teachers. Traditional interviewing processes are notoriously unreliable. If the approach is supported by enough stakeholders and is delivering results, it is more difficult for a new leader to undermine it, but not impossible. Constancy of dynamic leadership is very important for the continual development of stakeholding.

Stakeholding in the Education – Common Purpose

Many schools have been mandated to produce School Aims and Development Plans. Most are bland statements produced by a handful of senior staff. All of the schools mentioned in this book have set about a continuous process of involving all stakeholders in strategic planning.

Somervale Comprehensive School started its quality journey with a complete review, which included teachers, support staff, parents, students, employers and the senior management team. The result was a very clear statement of purpose, with agreed improvement priorities. In the initial phase, MEHS followed a similar process. Two years ago they carried out a re-visioning exercise for the school and the students. This time they incorporated drama. This was more fun and helped engage more people. Because of the continual turnover of students it is very important for schools to continually revisit strategy.

Smith's Wood School approached the issue of common purpose from a community perspective and worked very closely with the partner schools. Schools are at the heart of communities and very little improvement can be achieved in isolation. All have had to work hard to manifest their strategies on a day-to-day basis. The 'acid test' of a strategy is whether all the stakeholders find it meaningful for their contributions. This can only be achieved over time by structured dialogue.

Stakeholding in the Education – Suitable Skills

Schools have had to build their knowledge and expertise for stakeholding. As a generalisation educationalists seem to appreciate the values and principles instinctively. They often lack the methods, tools and techniques but learn them very rapidly. Teacher Training Colleges should be supporting future teachers by equipping them to work in this way.

In the UK the schools have tended to learn by doing. As they proceed they have trained up facilitators. The most successful schools have trained a broad cross-section of stakeholders, including students, at the same time. Because funds are extremely limited they have often had to do this with the support of leading employers. Frequently this support is given 'in kind' by offering facilities, materials and staff. Training and Enterprise Councils are in an ideal position to help with funding. Several of these schools have used funds for implementing Investors in People for training stakeholders. Many of the students who have been trained have gone on to use the experience to secure good jobs. MEHS has gone one stage further and made training in quality, teamwork, visioning and partnering, etc, central within the curriculum. All students learn common methods, tools and techniques, which are used subsequently in all lessons. This has improved productivity for all teachers and ensures that the students have a common 'toolkit'.

Many teachers who have been trained have taken the concepts straight into their classrooms. Students learn the methods very rapidly and tools like mind mapping can have major benefits in improving memory and creative thinking. In one school that faltered in the process, due to the departure of several key leaders at once, 50% of the teachers went on to more senior positions in other schools. In this way the expertise has spread across the education community.

Stakeholding in the Education – Continual Improvement

The principles and methods in this book seem to be applied at three levels in schools. The first, and possibly lowest level of application, is to the management processes of a school, or other educational establishment. Schools do have many processes in common with other organisations. They produce strategic plans, recruit and develop staff, deploy resources and require principle-centred leadership. Whilst this type of application can produce improvements in efficiency, it is unlikely to inspire students and teachers, and to deal with the real root issues which lie within the learning processes. The next level is the training of students. The philosophy, in its totality, needs to be covered along with methods and tools. This becomes more exciting because it enables the school to move to the highest level.

The highest level is where application impacts the classroom and all the learning processes. Todd Bergman, Quality Co-ordinator, MEHS defines the approach as a philosophy, supported by a comprehensive toolkit, driven by students and staff, in order to identify, analyse and remove the barriers to learning. One view of the teacher's role is to motivate students to learn. Another is for the teacher to work with the students to remove the barriers to motivation. All of us are born with an inherent love of learning and the 'forces of destruction' which are built into our systems, work to drive this out of us. Some of us are lucky enough to survive the system. The dramatic improvements are achieved when the school achieves this level of application. Few have got to this level.

MEHS has led in the transformation of learning. Students have been involved in driving the change right from day one. Early discussions with students highlighted the need to fundamentally change the school timetable. The young adults felt that a 40-minute lesson period was too long for 'chalk and talk' and too short for proper participation and reflection. The school redesigned the timetable around 90-minute learning periods. It now operates on a two-week cycle. This change freed an afternoon every two weeks which is used for learning the methods of quality improvement.

More profound change followed by involving the students in redesigning curriculum and assessment. Because the students are engaged in understanding why they are learning something, and in regular reviews of the curriculum, they are now directly influencing future curriculum as well as delivery. This is achieved through the use of competence-based learning and Bloom's taxonomy. A great deal of time is spent helping the students learn how to learn. The original curriculum, influenced by State guidelines and other reports about the type of skills that will be needed in the future, has been adapted to meet the local community's requirements.

Delivery of curriculum does not just happen in the classroom. It happens throughout the student's time at a school. Marty Johnson, Science Teacher at MEHS, refers to the kiss principle. Most people remember their first kiss. They do not remember when they first heard about kissing and were told how it is done! Learning must relate to application and so great effort is placed on cross-curricular projects.

Possibly the most controversial change at MEHS has been on the subject of assessment. Dr Deming taught about the harmful effects of grading and ranking, as well as depending on mass inspection. Applying his teachings to education, as MEHS have done, means monitoring learning, not controlling the students. The school uses the learning matrices and Bloom's taxonomy in order for students to assess their own learning. This is not done lightly. Students are taught 'learning theories' and assessment techniques. They have to document, demonstrate and defend their learning. The documentation ends up in extensive portfolios, soon to be put on CD ROMs.

For a variety of reasons most of the improvement in the UK has focused on the lower levels of application. One of the main reasons is the inability of schools to change one of their core processes – curriculum development – because of the National Curriculum. Other reasons include change overload and lack of resources. Another, more subtle one is the fear in schools of meaningfully engaging all the stakeholders.

Smith's Wood Schools have started to approach this head on. They have a process of partnership working that is looking at the root causes issues across the community. Forty students, aged eight to 14 were involved in the first workshop. They used tools and techniques to answer the following questions. What political, economic, social and technical changes in the next 20 years could profoundly influence your future? What skills and knowledge will you need to be successful in such an uncertain future? Where are the barriers in the existing education system, which could limit your future success? An incredible amount of issues were raised. The issues included the quality and consistency of teaching, parental support, lack of resources, bullying and health. The students' agenda was then used to direct a workshop for the adult stakeholders. This focused on raising and planning improvements to the root causes of the students' issues. These plans are currently being implemented across the community. Solutions included a process for identifying and sharing resources, a telephone help line for parents and joining forces for teacher training and development.

Lee Regan, Head teacher of St John the Baptist Primary School, has taken a very systemic approach to improving student performance. The staff believes that a major constraint to the performance of their children is the lack of parental support. These parents lack the confidence and skills to get actively involved in improvement. Over the last two years the school has been running basic adult education in First Aid. This gets the parents used to coming into the school and has given many of them a sense of achievement when they secure recognised qualifications. This has resulted in a steady improvement in the numbers attending parents' evenings. This might seem an indirect way of addressing the problem but it is getting to the root causes and will achieve sustainable improvements.

Stakeholding in the Education — Strong Relationships

The best examples of building strong relationships are from the Midlands. This work has been initiated by the Central England Education Business Partnership.

Rob Hawkins and Lee Regan have been working hard to establish strong partnerships. Both are forming strong working relationships founded on trust, respect and joint working. A great deal of preparation has been required to bring the representatives from partner schools, parents, governors, industry and the wider community together. A degree of trust is required to get the different stakeholders together in the same room. Both Head teachers have used a clear structure and way of working. The first stage has been to establish an agreed code of co-operation. When this has been breached, as it inevitably will be, the code has been enforced by all partners and corrective action taken. All of the work has centred on understanding each other's issues in an open and honest way. A problem for one partner group is likely to affect all so there has been a shared responsibility to work together to deal with the root causes. A great deal of time and effort has been spent arriving at a shared agenda and set of priorities. This has sometimes meant leaving personal agendas behind. Each partner has the right to say 'no deal' but this has rarely happened.

Building relationships takes time. It cannot be rushed. Partners have to be allowed to move at their own speed. Establishing joint agendas is only the first stage. The relationships must continue to be built over time. At any point there may be setbacks. It is useful to have a process for handling these potential conflicts. In these cases both schools have used an independent, external facilitator. Trust is not 'digital'. It varies on a scale from very low trust and suspicion through to very high levels of trust. It continues to be built by joint working, sharing and open communication. Trust takes years to build and can be damaged very easily. Partnerships need to monitor levels of trust continuously and do everything possible to prevent damage to this precious commodity.

Stakeholding in the Education — Sustainable Results

Much of the stakeholding work in education is in its formative stages. Most of the work has achieved short-term improvements, such as improved staff morale, better use of resources, more parent involvement, etc. MEHS has been on 'the journey' the longest and they have achieved the most dramatic improvements. This has taken nine years of hard work but the fundamental way the school works has changed. Some of the results achieved by Mt Edgecumbe are listed below:

- 68% of graduates continue onto college or university. Another 28% of graduates go to technical/trade school or into military service. The average progression rate to college for rural High Schools is below 5%.
- The dropout rate varies between zero and 0.5%.
- 97% of students believe that the quality of education received was better than available in their home communities.
- 92% of the 1992 graduates would like their children to attend. The academic challenge was cited as the main reason.
- 75% of graduates felt that the school did a good job preparing them for continuing education.
- Drug and alcohol abuse has fallen dramatically.
- Parent satisfaction has risen.

Most of the above information was not even collected prior to the improvements. Traditional SAT scores have improved slightly but MEHS believe that this is far too crude a tool to use in isolation and have consequently developed their own, additional measures of succcss. Schools must consider very early on by what means they are going to measure improvement.

Stakeholding in the Education – Sound Evaluation

In the early Nineties the British Government introduced major changes to the way schools are inspected. The Office of Standards in Education (OFSTED) was established and inspection was opened up to market forces, including lay people on inspection teams. Schools have to 'buy in' a full inspection every four years. This can be very expensive. The quality of inspection varies considerably depending on the attitudes of the Inspectors. Those that take an aggressive approach, based on fear, achieve little long-term improvement. The Inspectors that work in partnership, helping to highlight the real root cause problems, prove to be the most successful.

However, if inspection is going to be of value it must move away from being 'done to' the school and become part of the way the school runs normally. Some schools have appreciated this and have started to adopt frameworks for self-assessment. In the US the Baldrige Award is being used extensively by schools to monitor their improvement. In the UK leading schools are starting to adapt the EFQM's Business Excellence Model. Even OFSTED is starting to realise the ineffectiveness of infrequent external inspections and is starting to consider self-assessment. Figure 29 shows an adaptation of the BEM to a school environment.

It is predicted that this model will become a very common means of monitoring the overall progress of schools. Methods of self-assessment selected will depend on the degree of accuracy required and the associated costs. Thankfully the model requires the degree of stakeholder satisfaction to be monitored regularly.

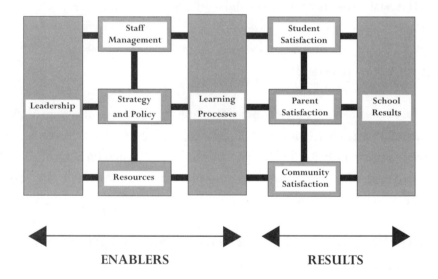

Figure 29. Business Excellence Model adapted for a school

Chapter 12

Stakeholding in Health Care

Health Care as a System

Having stressed the importance of systems thinking it is appropriate to start each of the chapters in this part of the book with an overview of the total system into which the organisations fit (Figure 30).

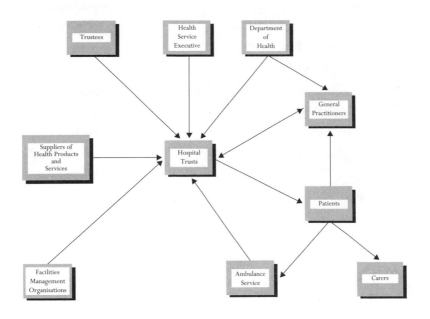

Figure 30. Health Care as a System

The Health Care System in the UK has undergone a profound transformation in the last ten years with the introduction of the 'Internal Market'. Unfortunately this has created a very legalistic form of partnership with purchasers of service contracting with providers. The new Government is currently reviewing the process. The aim is to create deeper, more meaningful partnerships, as defined in this book, and to reduce the incredible bureaucracy that has been created. The system is currently highly fragmented with all organisations 'doing their best'.

The purchasers, including General Practitioners and other Hospital Trusts, currently contract with the providers such as hospitals and ambulance services. The providers aim to provide good quality, affordable health care to patients, carers and the wider community. Everyone recognises the need to move from corrective to preventive forms of health care. There is endemic under-funding and existing funds are not used optimally. The National Health Service comprises many other types of service providers, such as facilities management organisations. Many of these have been subjected to market testing and some have been privatised. Service providers obviously purchase products and services from both the public and private sectors.

Background Information

The following examples are drawn for a range of UK health care providers including Hospital Trusts, Ambulance Services and Facilities Management Organisations. The Royal National Hospital for Rheumatic Diseases (RNHRD) is a centre for excellence in Rheumatology and head injuries. This small hospital has a long history and is based in Bath because of the presence of the spa. The RNHRD employs around 400 staff and has a worldwide reputation. CAPITEC, also in Bath, was launched in 1991 as a part of the Bath Mental Health Care NHS Trust in order to become the model for Estates Management for the NHS. Their growth has been impressive. It has been founded on the principles of stakeholding and partnership. The East Wiltshire Community and Mental Health Trust (EWCMHT) is another Hospital Trust. They provide a range of health services in East Wiltshire. They too have been trying to form strong partnerships with other agencies, customers and suppliers. Avon Ambulance Service covers the whole of the County formerly known as Avon. They cover urban areas such as Bristol and Bath as well as many dispersed rural communities. All of these organisations are customers and suppliers of each other and have provided a good opportunity to work on the whole health care system in this region.

Stakeholding in Health Care — Effective Leadership

The success of CAPITEC and RNHRD, in particular, is founded on very sound leadership. Both David Lawrence, Chief Executive of CAPITEC and Nicola Carmichael, Chief Executive of RNHRD, have strong beliefs in the importance of partnerships to improve the quality of health services. Both individuals have very personal reasons for wanting to provide excellent health care. They could easily earn higher salaries in the private sector but they are passionate about what they do in very different ways. They also have very different styles of leadership but with common underpinning principles. Firstly they are always receptive to new ideas, checking them very carefully. Once committed to principles, they invest their own time to learn with their stakeholders, in particular their staff. Both are self-confident enough to admit their own weaknesses and failings but practise visible, continual learning. They would be the first to admit that they have a long way to go, but recognise that they have to value, respect and use the expertise within their partnerships. Both are committed but do not take themselves too seriously. They have very well developed senses of humour and put all stakeholders at their ease. They are not 'glory boys' and instil a strong sense of loyalty for the good of the organisation.

Kevin Dougherty, newly appointed Chief Executive of the Avon Ambulance Trust, inherited a staff that was highly de-motivated. One of his first actions was to spend considerable time observing on the ambulances. This created no end of goodwill as well as a depth of understanding and appreciation. All three of these executives spend considerable time with all their stakeholders and keep their feet firmly on the ground. In CAPITEC's case it has been very much the supplier driving improvement and raising the expectations of the customers.

All three leaders try to lead by example and do not flit from one initiative to another. All have committed to Investors in People, the UK standard of best practice for people development. CAPITEC was one of the first organisations in health care to achieve the standard. They have also achieved ISO9000 certification in a practical and beneficial way. These people understand how these initiatives fit into the bigger picture of transformation. All three organisations are now busy implementing continual improvement with their stakeholders.

To these leaders their main role is to enable or facilitate their stakeholders to improve their products, services and processes. They are working to remove the barriers that rob people of their right to pride in work through the allocation or time and training. In the end it is not their words that matter but their actions.

Stakeholding in Health Care – Common Purpose

The best example of engaging stakeholders in strategic planning comes from CAPITEC. They took a risk by attempting to do their Corporate and Business Planning in a very different way to others. The process started with a strategic review with a range of staff. This led to the development of a model of the process, incorporating all the key stakeholders, along with factors critical for success. At the conclusion of this one-day review it was decided to try to engage all the stakeholders in the process. A subsequent series of workshops was organised.

The first involved all staff in the formulation of a statement of purpose including value statements. In mixed groups the staff then produced their own Critical Success Factors. Then in pairs they identified how their own work directly contributes to the achievement of the CSFs. There were many other benefits of this workshop. It was the first time that all the staff had worked in such a structured and focused way. There were many new members of staff who benefited by working with others and by rapidly understanding where the organisation was headed. The overall feedback was very positive.

The second workshop involved a range of customers in defining and prioritising their wants and needs. They then evaluated how well CAPITEC was performing against these criteria. This work led to the creation of a structured questionnaire that was used informally by the Chief Executive, and other senior managers, to conduct client reviews. This enabled a greater number of customers to be involved. The work assisted the organisation in identifying customer-focused innovations. It also enhanced existing and potential customer relationships by building CAPITEC's reputation as a customer-driven organisation.

The third workshop involved a very diverse cross-section of partners, including lawyers, building contractors and consultancy firms. This review focused on identifying the factors critical for strong supplier partnerships and produced plans for creating them. In response CAPITEC set up an improvement team to redesign its supplier selection process. This is now based on the Business Excellence Model, which is much broader than the previous criteria.

Shortly after the workshops the three-year business plan was produced. It is succinct and focused and received praise from CAPITEC's Parent Trust. This process is now being repeated and improved each year. The key factor is the amount of ownership and understanding. It may have taken longer to produce but it means something to the majority of the stakeholders, unlike many of the worthless documents produced by other organisations. There was a potential 'spanner the works'. When CAPITEC was formed there was an agreement that the organisation would be 'market tested'. With the change of government it seemed that to go through the process was potentially a waste of time. In response David Lawrence invited all the stakeholders, including the National Health Service Executive, to a facilitated workshop. A potentially damaging conflict was averted and the partners agreed a sensible approach that would not waste taxpayers' money. As an indirect consequence CAPITEC is now likely to merge with what was seen as its main competitor in the North of England. This is an example of co-operation, not mindless competition. The three-year contract, awarded as a consequence, has tough service and cost reduction goals. These can only be safely achieved through stakeholder partnerships.

Summary of CAPITEC's future direction.

Vision — we aim to be the first choice provider of management services to the NHS.

Mission — we will achieve our mission by working in partnership to provide and continually improve management services that anticipate and exceed the needs and wants of our clients.

Values — we believe:
- in public sector values in a culture of enterprise.
- that the needs and wants of our clients come first.
- our success will facilitate improvements in the delivery of health and social care.
- that every member of our staff is uniquely important to our success.

Factors critical to the success of the business:

1 Support of our parent organisation.
2 Client satisfaction.
3 Business development.
4 Business results.
5 Effective leadership and robust management systems.
6 Staff satisfaction.
7 Marketing.
8 Impact on the NHS.

The detailed plans are structured around these Critical Success Factors with supporting information such as proposed services, financial performance and forecasts and competitor and risk analysis.

Stakeholding in Health Care – Suitable Skills

All the organisations have had to build their capacity for managing partnerships and driving process improvement. Most have trained a wide cross-section of staff to be confident and competent to facilitate teams of stakeholders to improve core processes. These people have learnt the methods, tools and techniques of improvement as well as softer skills such as how to manage conflict and achieve consensus. Real projects are central to the learning experience, improving the translation of theory into practice and delivering early benefits as well.

The facilitators are then used as a central resource to co-ordinate improvements throughout the health care system. They develop a sense of 'profound knowledge' and hone their skills and particular styles of facilitation. Many of these people have enhanced their careers by gaining these skills and by using them on a day-to-day basis as well. It is satisfying to experience their confidence and self-esteem improving. Having a core resource of facilitators creates a readiness to build strong stakeholder partnerships.

The RNHRD also developed an introduction for all staff. These sessions bring together trustees, doctors, administrators, nurses and support staff such as porters into one learning environment. Not only does this raise awareness, but also through active participation, these stakeholders learn to value each other's opinions and views.

Stakeholding in Health Care – Continual Improvement

The examples of continual improvement in these organisations are already legion. Some of the more interesting or challenging examples are included.

One such example is from the RNHRD. Due to government pressure all Trusts have had to subject their support services, such as catering and portering, to market testing. This has created fear in the staff and led to private sector companies taking over many services, in theory providing better quality services at lower cost. The onus was on the Trusts to demonstrate that their services were providing best value. Actually, the real issue was lowest cost not necessarily best value for money. The RNHRD had employed consultant to evaluate the support services. They had used traditional methods and the work had not been successful. It was decided to use a facilitative approach with the stakeholders.

The purpose of the work was to review the organisation of support services to ensure: the highest levels of patient care, best use of resources and the highest levels of job satisfaction. The review was to cover the porters, domestics, auxiliary nurses and therapy helpers. A 'contract' was agreed between the management team and the representatives doing the work. No one was to be made redundant as a result of the review but they may have to be prepared to work in different ways, with training and support being provided. The management team agreed to implement the recommendations as long as sound evidence was provided for the conclusions. Finally, the management team agreed to provide the time and the space for the team to follow a rigorous process. The team did their work over three day-long workshops with surveys and data collection in between.

Firstly they clarified the existing roles and responsibilities of the support staff. The customers' wants and needs were defined and agreed. The representatives then identified the barriers in the existing organisation that prevented the provision of high quality, low cost service. The rest of the time was spent exploring alternative ways of organising and then producing recommendations.

The main benefit of this work is that it put the responsibility for reviewing with the people who do the work. It was customer-focused and led to many innovative ideas. In the end the staff had to take responsibility for the consequences of their proposals. Most importantly goodwill was restored and the ideas were implemented quickly and effectively with high levels of ownership.

Another initiative in the EWCMHT focused on the provision of child health services, particularly Case Conferences. The quality of this process can be a matter of life or death. In one tragic case in another part of the country, an administrative error contributed to the death of a child through abuse. In this process internal stakeholders including nurses, administrators and doctors have to work in partnership with other agencies such as schools and social services. The partners, for the first time, flowcharted the whole Case Conference Process. They collected data concerning cancellations and postponements and then analysed the root cause problems. They generated a series of improvements, in partnership, which has resulted in better communication, more rapid decisions and better administration.

CAPITEC followed a similar approach to continual improvement. They wished to ensure that their supplier selection process ensured complete confidence in suppliers. They too analysed the existing process and decided to adopt a much more holistic and rigorous process of selection. They based this on the Business Excellence Model. It was decided that they had to lead by example so the improvements are being phased in over a period of time, which allows CAPITEC to demonstrate its own commitment to best practice. It also enabled them to integrate the benefit of suppliers that were already ISO9000 and IIP certified.

A major constraint in all the health care work has been engaging the medical profession. Without them any approach to improvement is very limited. Getting doctors involved is critical but very difficult. It is too easy to resort to traditional stereotypes and blame them for arrogance and lack of interest. The main issues centred on lack of time, poor training and fear of revealing lack of knowledge. Some doctors were particularly concerned about involving patients. They needed to be convinced that the benefits outweigh the potential disadvantages. Where doctors have been actively involved, as yet another key stakeholder group, the benefits have been profound.

Stakeholding in Health Care – Strong Relationships

One of the main benefits of the joint training and improvement work has been the less tangible development of better working relationships. It is hard, if not impossible, to quantify this numerically. In all the organisations barriers have started to come down. Across agencies misunderstandings have diminished as a result of people starting to understand the constraints that each of them work under. As the teams have developed they have started to be much more honest with each other. A breakthrough came in the RNHRD when the doctors really opened up about their concerns. It was a brave move and was respected by the other stakeholders present. In some cases there have been real tensions, especially when hidden agendas are suspected. In the case of the RNHRD's initiative on support services it was known by the staff that one or two senior managers favoured dispersing the porters to the wards. The porters were very concerned. However, the 'contract' provided some comfort and when the groups realised that the senior management team was really going to accept their ideas, a great deal of trust was created, with many other spin-off benefits.

A major constraint has been the legalistic nature of the internal market in the NHS. This is based on very simplistic measures which sometimes undermine qualitative work. If true partnerships are going to be created we need to move from conflict-based contracts to a position of shared responsibility. All the improvement work that directly involved the contractors or purchasers helped develop these relationships. With a new government that wishes to move in this direction many of the contractual constraints should be removed.

Stakeholding in Heath Care – Sustainable Results

All the organisations have experienced less tangible improvements in morale and understanding. Many can show tangible improvements in patient care and satisfaction. Some of the work has led directly to cost savings through the removal of duplication and the introduction of better ways of working.

The most outstanding results have been achieved by CAPITEC. Based on the application of the principles of stakeholding they have quadrupled their turnover and increased their return to the Parent Trust. They are on the verge of 'merging' with their main competitor and look set to dominate their market, taking them towards their vision. A key issue is maintaining and building on their culture as they go through rapid growth in size. They understand this risk and already have plans in place to deal with the staff expansion. They have to achieve tough targets on cost reduction but they have built the capacity to achieve these targets in meaningful ways.

Stakeholding in Health Care – Sound Evaluation

Each organisation has been encouraged to design evaluation throughout the stakeholding process. Methods vary from regular, informal reviews through to rigorous self-assessment. Good strategic planning, driven by customers' wants and needs, has enabled the organisations to develop 'dashboards'. These are based on statistical methods and provide sound evidence of improvements in critical areas.

Both CAPITEC and RNHRD have adopted the Business Excellence Model for complete business evaluation. They are in the early stages of using the framework and assessments have tended to be informal and not particularly accurate. As their confidence and knowledge of the methods of self-assessment grow they will probably introduce more rigorous and regular reviews engaging a wider group of stakeholders.

Chapter 13

Stakeholding in Government Agencies, Quangos and the Voluntary Sector

Agencies, Quangos and the Voluntary Sector as a System

Having stressed the importance of systems thinking it is appropriate to start each of the Chapters in this part of the book with an overview of the total system into which the organisations fit (Figure 31).

The number of government-funded agencies and quangos has increased dramatically due to the previous Conservative administration. Many services that were supplied by public sector organisations are now delivered by autonomous agencies. Many are limited by guarantee and form a new part of the economy that is neither truly part of the public nor private sectors. This 'twilight zone' has inherited many of the difficulties of both sectors. They do not have the freedom of private companies to select their own core products and services and are subjected to stringent and restrictive controls. The idea behind their formation was to give greater flexibility and more accountability for quality and costs.

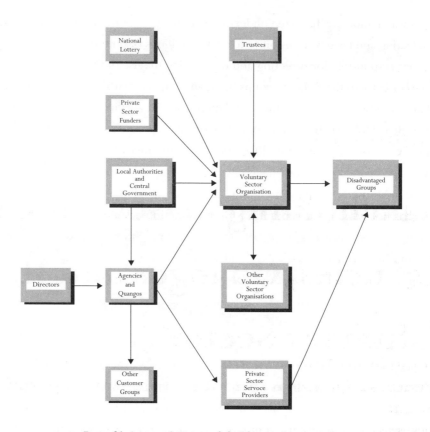

Figure 31. Agencies, Quangos and the Voluntary Sector as a System

The range of services provided by agencies and quangos is vast. They exist in the military right through to education and health care. They all contract with the relevant government departments to provide services. These are usually precisely defined and controlled with operating contracts. Unfortunately the civil service cannot resist the temptation to monitor and control in inflexible, simplistic and bureaucratic ways. They emphasise numerical outputs often at the expense of less quantifiable outcomes. The funders often demand the kind of causality that even the Stock Market would find impossible to prove. One of the agendas of creating agencies was to subject them to market forces, and some have found that shortly after creation they have been replaced with private sector suppliers. Quangos tend to be governed by Boards of Directors. Senior posts are usually political and undemocratic. For every known Labour sympathiser on Boards there are 17 Tories! Few people appreciate the sinister way in which local democracy has been undermined in the name of efficiency. Boards are often self-selecting and have responsibility for many millions of pounds of public funds. These teams are responsible for directing and monitoring the use of funds. They often provide services directly to their client groups but many contract with private sector companies.

The voluntary sector has more independence in service delivery. A charity will have a Board of Trustees and will deliver services to disadvantaged groups. The voluntary sector is a major employer in the community and must be taken seriously. They can be prone to being managed by 'the great and the good' but many are working to be more representative, including service users on their Boards. The voluntary sector has not got a good reputation for working in partnership with others, but this is changing. They are in danger of becoming supply rather than customer-driven. However, they have a great deal of goodwill and expertise to be mobilised. Their funds can come from local and national government, private sector companies and new initiatives like the National Lottery. Agencies and quangos often need to work closely with their voluntary sector colleagues.

Background Information

The examples are drawn from a wide range of agencies, quangos and charities. The Surrey Care Trust is an innovative organisation that provides a wide range of multi-agency services to different groups of vulnerable people throughout Surrey. It is a unique partnership of ten agencies drawn from statutory, independent and commercial sectors. The partnership includes probation, social services, the church, police, health, housing, voluntary sector, business community, education and the magistracy. The Trust have formed strong relationships with private companies including prestigious firms such as Toshiba.

The Army Technical Support Agency provides specialist procurement advice, guidance and support to the Armed Forces. They have recently become a fully-fledged agency and have been determined to show that they can provide as good value for money as any private company. Impartiality is important in their work and it would be hard to imagine a scenario whereby they were wholly-owned by a Defence Original Equipment Manufacturer.

Training and Enterprise Councils were formed in the early Nineties throughout England and Wales to provide services to unemployed people and employers in order to improve local competitiveness. They are responsible for managing government training and retraining programmes as well as innovative initiatives for employers such as Investors in People. TECs have tended to become contract managers for other organisations such as Business Links, Regeneration Partnerships and private sector training providers. The government of the day insisted that the TEC Boards comprised 75% of leaders from local business. Other representatives come from education and the voluntary sector. TECs were modelled on PICs from the US. New Labour is not convinced of their real benefits and is currently reviewing their role. Labour is most concerned about lack of public accountability for funds. Many of the initial directors from business have become disillusioned about the degree of freedom that they were offered. TECs, like many other quangos, have been subjected to many bureaucratic monitoring systems. At the last count TECs were being monitored by up to five different and incompatible quality systems. A successful angler cannot afford to keep removing the line to check the bait every five minutes. He or she will catch nothing, but this is sometimes how it feels with government auditing and monitoring. Balancing public accountability and commercial freedom is a real challenge for governments wanting to improve service delivery.

Stakeholding in Agencies and the Voluntary Sector – Effective Leadership

One of the best examples of leadership is from the Surrey Care Trust. Penny Rkaina is the Chief Executive. Penny leads with an energy and determination that is enviable. She is determined that SCT adopts the best practices of modern management without damaging the caring culture that is paramount. This has led to many 'spin off' benefits, not least of which is improved reputation with potential 'blue chip' funders. These companies expect the same kind of professionalism and focus from the organisations that they fund that they themselves would demand. One of the challenges the SCT faces is how to provide continuity when so many key staff are on short-term secondments from other partner organisations. This places extra demand on induction, strategic planning and sustaining the culture. Penny has adopted many of the best practices from industry in strategic planning. Process Owners have clear key objectives and are given high levels of empowerment to achieve them. The values and principles of the organisation are regularly reviewed and once agreed are non-negotiable. SCT is leading the way in transforming the culture of the voluntary sector. They are focused on the demand not supply side and are set to continue to grow in services, funds and reputation.

Stakeholding in Agencies and the Voluntary Sector – Common Purpose

One TEC invested considerable energy in achieving a shared sense of purpose. This is highly important because many of the government programmes appear to be fragmented. At last count it has at least 50 major partners from all sectors of the community. Any one of the half a million residents and workers of their area could be multiple customers of services.

In 1991 the senior managers set about identifying critical processes. In a facilitated workshop the long-term vision and goals were related back to existing and potential services. Many interesting anomalies were highlighted. Firstly some of the most favoured processes had minimal impacts on the critical success factors. As a result one or two programmes were abandoned. Some of the weaker managers were responsible for the more critical processes. Responsibilities were revised as a consequence. This strategic planning process has been applied continually and improved after each application. In the first year too few stakeholders were included. Subsequent applications have involved all staff, key partners, directors and inputs from customers from surveys and public meetings.

A key task has been managing the complexity of the overall task. There are many customers and other stakeholders. Each has many wants and needs, each of which has many indicators. One year the organisation nearly stalled trying to link process indicators to organisational indicators to community-wide indicators. Stringent prioritising had to be introduced based on the 80/20 principle. (Twenty percent of the indicators provide 80% of the information.) Unfortunately, the Department for Education and Employment has imposed many less suitable indicators. Many of the more critical indicators are subjective or qualitative.

When the TEC was audited against the Investors in People standard, the Assessor identified the high degree of common purpose. This task has been made even more challenging by the creation of separate satellite companies. The TEC believes that the only way to get real partnership is to create organisations where strategy and delivery are shared. It now guides, funds and monitors The Learning Partnership West, The Western Development Partnership, Business Link West and The Equality Foundation. The result has been better partnership working, more customer focus and improved value for money. The big challenge is preventing fragmentation. The TEC's role is now that of a strategic convenor. The need for common purpose is now even greater.

All the work on strategic planning has led to a succinct one-page summary. The Vision, collective prosperity and individual success, is supported by the Mission Statement. This is 'through partnership to support organisations and individuals to achieve their full potential'. To achieve the Vision and Mission there are seven Strategic Objectives. They are:

1. Development of a Shared Economic Strategy — through partnership and influence secure agreement and delivery of the economic development strategy.

2. Stimulating Business Success - help businesses succeed (with particular emphasis on the development of managers and other staff).

3. Individuals - encourage life-long learning and supported by guidance, promote raised levels of expectation and achievement in education, training and employment.

4. Business, Education and Training - improve shared understanding, collaboration and joint action between business, education and training.

5. Empowering those who face disadvantage - enable those who face disadvantage to gain access to jobs, training and education by focusing on best practice in training, education and employment.

6. Resources - use our expertise to attract, allocate and manage resources from government and other sources to meet, together with our partners, the priorities identified in our plans.

7. Pre-requisite Objective - continue to develop effective and competent staff, management and partnerships, informed by quality market intelligence.

The main processes and corresponding services are then linked to the Strategic Objectives using a simple table. Each Process Owner identifies, in their own planning process, how their work contributes to the achievement of these objectives. This planning document is central to regular staff appraisals.

Recently, after a Business Excellence Review, it was decided to document the Corporate Values. This was done in full consultation with all staff by a team of stakeholders. There are eight core values:

1. A collective drive for business success and excellence.
2. Teamwork.
3. Empowered individuals.
4. Openness, honesty and straightforwardness.
5. Enjoyment.
6. Inclusive approach based on stakeholding.
7. Equal and fair opportunities.
8. Engagement with the local community.

The real value of the statements is not the words but what they mean in the hearts and minds of the stakeholders. Do these statements have any relevance to stakeholders on a day-to-day basis? It they don't they become platitudes.

Stakeholding in Agencies and the Voluntary Sector – Suitable Skills

Another TEC, responsible for the County of Essex, has taken a very systematic approach to developing suitable skills. They have adopted the principles and practices of Investors in People to develop a range of programmes. Members of staff, who have broad remits involving many stakeholders, have been trained as Facilitators. They have all completed extensive projects to demonstrate their competence. These people are now used as an internal and external resource on critical projects. All staff go through an introductory session on the values and ways of working adopted by Essex TEC. They now have the capacity to sustain effective stakeholding.

Stakeholding in Agencies and the Voluntary Sector – Continual Improvement

In the early Nineties it was decided by government ministers to create a new agency out of the Technical Branches that formed the Director General Equipment Support of the British Army. The plan was to integrate control under one Chief Executive and to relocate onto one site. In 1995 the Army Technical Support Agency (ATSA) was created. ATSA provides a range of technical services to the Armed Services including advice on procurement, maintenance, training and engineering modifications. In preparation for becoming an agency the staff of ATSA had carried out extensive customer surveys. They also produced extensive process models of the existing organisation. ATSA's aim is to enhance the Army's operational capability by providing an effective and efficient technical support service. Engineering excellence is central to their success along with close links to the users of the equipment.

The changes presented other opportunities. Consultation with stakeholders highlighted the possibilities of re-engineering the core processes at the same time as becoming an agency and relocating. A steering group was formed to ensure a fully integrated business. The ATSA Change Team's (ACT) purpose was to drive the change process forward, in line with best practice, ensuring implementation on time. Key processes were identified for improvement and Process Improvement Groups (PIGs) were established. Early teams addressed task management, the influence of equipment design, provision of tools and test equipment and support equipment. The teams followed the process improvement cycle (see Figure 13) with the aim of finding quantum improvements through integration of resources. Stakeholders were involved throughout. This structured approach allowed ATSA to manage a very large amount of change. The integration provided 'one-off' opportunities to profoundly change the way the old organisation had operated.

Stakeholding in Agencies and the Voluntary Sector – Strong Relationships

One TEC has used the principles of quality and stakeholding both at the organisational and process levels. There are many examples of how the organisation has engaged stakeholders at the start of service and process design. One such example concerned the development of a process to help a large employer handle a major redundancy.

The company approached the TEC confidentially. It had to make large-scale redundancies and wanted to make the process as painless as possible for its staff. After high level discussions the TEC formed a development team with the Employment Service, Careers Service and the Company. Within a matter of weeks a service was developed which built on the existing strengths of the partners to ensure that both employees' and the employer's wants and needs were met. The results impressed all stakeholders and highlighted the need to continue to work in this way.

After a lot of initial suspicion the TEC has come to a point whereby the same approach is being applied to Government Training Programmes. Existing providers of service were very wary of the TEC, the 'new kid on the block'. Over a period of several years the levels of trust have been built up to a point where the different suppliers regularly meet to review strategy and operational problems. The barriers are being demolished by getting all players to focus externally on the wants and needs of the people they serve. It has taken time for the stakeholders to feel safe in being honest about the real problems, to address the underlying processes and to avoid blaming each other. A key development was the introduction of joint training programmes on quality and stakeholding. Unfortunately this coincided with particularly painful contract reviews. Over time the TEC has tried to move away from a legalistic, contractual partnership to a deeper relationship. This has been constrained by the conflict approach used by Central Government. A sense of realism has emerged by understanding the difficulties of each of the suppliers in the process.

The TEC has recently secured new funds under the new government's Welfare to Work Programme. The purpose is to bridge the gap between the long-term unemployed people and the new job opportunities in developing organisations. Right at the start the Project Manager has requested facilitation support to bring all the stakeholders together for two one-day workshops. On the first day the attendees will agree the requirements of the employers and the unemployed people. They will then analyse why in the past it has proven difficult to match the two. On the second day, two weeks later, the attendees will work on new and improved ways of addressing the root cause problems. The workshops are being supported by research from academic researchers and with examples of best practice from other areas and countries. It is hoped that this way of working will be continued throughout the Project.

Another example of good relationships is explored in the section on community. The trouble-stricken Quality in the Community Project was only able to start to redress its problems because the individual stakeholders were able to state their concerns in an open, honest and productive way. This would not have been possible without the development of sound personal and organisational relationships.

Stakeholding in Agencies and the Voluntary Sector – Sustainable Results

Achieving short-term results is all too easy. Often the Hawthorn Effect is experienced. Just by making an intervention improvements are experienced. Making results sustainable is very difficult in agency, quango and voluntary sector work. These types of organisations must not lose sight of the fact that the funding Department is also a 'customer'. Unfortunately civil servants often select simplistic and short-term measures. These often measure outputs not real outcomes.

One TEC learnt the hard way by focusing on the communities' wants and needs rather than governmental measures. This led to highly innovative approaches, which were popular with the real beneficiaries of the services. However, over time it led to poor league table performance. Now it regards the government's measures as an absolute minimum, no matter how irrelevant. The TEC has supplemented these indicators with more useful and appropriate measures. Mt Edgecumbe High School had a similar experience. The State demands that standardised test scores be reported. These are not used internally to drive improvement. The real indicators are student progression into higher education and satisfying jobs, parent, student and teacher satisfaction. Few schools measure these results.

One of the biggest challenges agencies, quangos and voluntary organisations face is bridging the gap between the funders' measures and the real customers' wants and needs without falling into the trap of manipulating people and processes.

Stakeholding in Agencies and the Voluntary Sector – Sound Evaluation

The TEC mentioned above committed to use recognised models for assessing progress on its formation in 1991. Initially the priority was to achieve the Investors in People standard. Subsequently the Business Excellence Model was adopted for full-scale assessment of progress. In the early days very crude methods of self-assessment were used. The first approach was based on a very simple questionnaire that was given to senior managers. Interestingly, those managers who knew least about improvement scored themselves the highest. Those who had really understood the magnitude of the task tended, correctly, to score themselves low. These early exercises helped build up management knowledge and understanding of self-assessment so that they became convinced of the benefits of using more rigorous methods. Each year the TEC carries out a full self-assessment. All members of staff are now fully involved and it is planned to directly involve other stakeholders.

As the organisation has progressed it has become necessary to get some external validation. The British Quality Foundation now offers a service called Valid Score. The organisation presents its portfolio and self-assessment results to a team of two external, fully qualified assessors. They then test and validate the results. If the organisation achieves a certain score it is entitled to use a BQF logo stating the level achieved.

The Department for Education and Employment is now considering using the BEM to integrate the plethora of quality controls that it currently uses on TECs. This will reduce the cost of inspection whilst providing a degree of assurance. The early signs are that some Civil Servants are loath to move from external inspection to a process founded more on self- assessment. Asking people who have a vested interest in control, whether effective or not, to consider new ways of doing things is somewhat optimistic. The possible outcome is that there will be yet another inspection regime to add to the existing list.

The above TEC has, over the last five years, become reasonably sophisticated in self-assessment. There have been many direct benefits. It has forced the organisation to be more rigorous in demonstrating improvement by providing actual results rather than anecdotes. It has enabled reasonable reliable comparisons with other TECs and other organisations. Most importantly, because the model is based on excellence, it reduces the risks of complacency. BEM highlights how much has been achieved but shows clearly how much more is to be done.

Chapter 14

Community-wide Stakeholding

The Community as a System

Figure 9 shows a systems view of a community. Communities are inherently very complex to analyse. Processes cut right across them involving different stakeholders at different times. Martin Sandbrook, Head of Strategy for Western Training and Enterprise Council, has suggested that there are nine core processes that make up a city environment. These are:

1. Sheltering.
2. Moving around.
3. Obtaining goods.
4. Earning.
5. Entertainment.
6. Maintaining health.
7. Maintaining security.
8. Learning.
9. Administration.

Drawing an exact boundary around each process is not possible because they interrelate in complex and sometimes subtle ways. Bringing stakeholders together, particularly at the boundaries, can achieve dramatic improvements. The spread of quality principles, based on stakeholding throughout the whole system, has been referred to as Quality in the Community.

As with any new initiative, the work tends to be fragmented and exploratory. Many organisations across the UK and US are experimenting with the concepts and tools of quality in the community. There is no clear pattern, as a variety of organisations take the lead in their communities. Sometimes enlightened businesses take the lead; at other times it is innovative local authorities. Schools can be natural 'hubs' in the community. Other catalysts include Training and Enterprise Councils, the police and voluntary organisations.

Background Information

An interesting application of the principles of quality in the community was by the Safer Surrey Partnership. Surrey County Council and the Surrey Police formed this organisation to bring together stakeholders working on crime prevention and the achievement of safer communities. The chief executive, Annie Courtney, was impressed by the concepts and tools of total quality as applied to a whole community, in particular the integral consultation processes for improving the delivery of county services to the public. Through the Safer Surrey Partnership serious resources were committed.

A local businessman, Simon Wilsher, who runs the Wilsher Group and the Chief Executive of Reigate and Banstead Council initiated another approach in Surrey. Other business-led approaches have developed in Sheffield, Leeds and Bradford. In the US many areas have formed Community Quality Councils to promote and support systems thinking. In Bristol it was decided to take a 'grass roots' approach, working through existing agencies and voluntary organisations. The Quality in the Community (QIC) Project formed part of the city's successful bid for regeneration funds. Chattanooga in the States has been very successful in engaging stakeholders in visioning and priority setting. The approach was adopted by the Choices for Bristol Project, which is feeding into QIC. Some schools have been catalysts as well. Rodillian High School, near Leeds, involved 200 students, staff and community members in working on processes that affect their town.

Stakeholding in Communities – Effective Leadership

The Bristol QIC initiative was formulated in 1995. Initial meetings with the partners were very sensitive and exploratory. There was enough interest to proceed and to enter the project under the innovation category of the Single Regeneration Budget. Getting initial agreement at the start was relatively straightforward. Maintaining support was not. The Project is based on facilitating community stakeholders through defining their wants and needs, analysing the barriers to achieving them and then getting them to generate their own improvements. This is much more than traditional consultation. The community drives the whole improvement cycle. Secondary benefits include the skills and confidence that are transferred to the participants.

The first major hurdle was trying to engage the community directly. Communities often have self-appointed leaders. They may find this approach threatening because it could highlight that they are not as 'in touch' as they like to think. Voluntary organisations may discover that demand for their services is limited and that they have become 'supply driven'. This minefield of potential conflict was exacerbated by the first Project Manager's leadership style. His approach was too confrontational and dogmatic. People felt that they were being bulldozed and many felt that the principles were inappropriate.

It became very obvious that the project was in difficulty. A new Project Manager took over and immediately instigated a 'hearts and souls' reflection on the problems. All the key stakeholders were involved in personal reviews of the approach and the barriers. This time-consuming but valuable process led to renewed enthusiasm and generated many sound ideas. This group identified the key problems as lack of respect for cultural differences and poor initial communication. As a result the people involved have agreed to form a leadership body, spreading the responsibility for co-ordination. They have also generated excellent ideas to make the approach more culturally specific and to improve communication with some of the most disaffected members of the communities. Having a sensitive, respectful leadership style is critical. Many people have years of experience of these communities and they need to be engaged. Secondly it is easy to get support when funds are being offered, but keeping approaches going requires tenacious and reflective leadership.

Stakeholding in Communities – Common Purpose

The Choices for Bristol Project set out to emulate the successful visioning process used by communities in the US such as Chattanooga and New Haven. Its aim was to create a shared vision with agreed priorities. In the Project's own words 'Choices for Bristol is about you being heard. It's about talking with friends, colleagues and neighbours and putting your ideas forward as to how you think Bristol could become a better place to live. It's about bringing all those ideas together to build a powerful shared vision for Bristol's future and its about working together to make our vision reality.' The person who initiated the project, Karl Berger, gained support from business, local government, agencies and the voluntary sector. The Steering Committee was independent and non-partisan.

A local newspaper agreed to print an extensive eight-page 'pull out'. This explained the process, gave facts about Bristol and presented some alternative scenarios. People were encouraged to form groups and to submit their ideas. There was a help line to provide further support. The volunteer project workers also took the concept out to the communities, in particular schools, shopping centres and community centres. The ideas were then collated into themes. There were then a series of events in which volunteers facilitated attendees to collate and sort the ideas. A vision booklet was then produced and circulated widely. It is intend to set up improvement groups to implement the ideas generated.

The vision document was structured around six categories: acting together, people, places, play, work and transport. These categories were each broken down into sub-categories such as civic pride, crime, city economy, etc. The feedback from those that attended was very positive but participation was low; 2032 ideas were collected from a population of 0.5 million. Whilst the principle was sound other processes have to be used to ensure greater involvement. It would be too easy for elected members to discount the results as unrepresentative. Bristol is not a homogeneous community and maybe smaller districts should have been selected.

Stakeholding in Communities – Suitable Skills

Capacity building is a frequently used term in community development. It is essential that people have the confidence and skills to partake in any stakeholder initiatives. However, it is the responsibility of any co-ordinating body to make sure that all barriers are removed. Not making the process culturally specific leads to great problems. People from middle class, Anglo-Saxon backgrounds are developing most initiatives. These may be seen as alien and irrelevant by peoples of very different ethnic backgrounds. To combat this QIC is planning to make use of other tools to engage people such as art and drama and to use respected community elders as facilitators. Some approaches appear too 'managerial' for some. Language is also a potential barrier. Technical jargon should be avoided and languages other than English may have to be used. Physical barriers can often exist. Can people with disabilities be equally involved? Does the time of day prevent single mothers from attending?

The opportunity to get new skills is often a good incentive for people from disadvantaged backgrounds to get involved. In one Housing Estate in Plymouth the residents astonished themselves by taking over the management of the site. For years they had been patronisingly told that only the experts could do the work. Now the experts serve the management group which serves the residents. It is a good idea to try to link this kind of capacity building into a nationally recognised qualification. QIC intends to make their facilitator training compatible to National Vocational Qualifications. If people cannot be recognised through qualifications other appropriate means will have to be found. At the end of the day people have to do it for themselves and the role of the expert is to guide, train, coach and mentor so that he or she is no longer needed.

Stakeholding in Communities – Continual Improvement

The Safer Surrey Partnership's first approach was to bring together 150 stakeholders from across Surrey to explore the opportunities offered by quality principles and tools. This two-day event involved local politicians, senior police officers (Metropolitan and Surrey Police), teachers, social workers, planners, residents, representatives from voluntary organisations, etc. The event was highly interactive and consisted of a lot of group work.

To start the delegates identified the 'customers' of the crime prevention and community safety work. This list included the elderly, young people and businesses. In small groups they brainstormed and prioritised the particular 'wants and needs' of these customer groups. During the two days a vision and mission were generated and factors critical for success were listed.

On the second day delegates worked in small teams on specific problems such as truancy, leisure provision for young people and reducing the fear of crime experienced by the elderly. In multi-disciplinary teams, the groups brainstormed causes of these problems, identified root causes and generated solutions. The debates were very revealing and delegates concluded that this approach had to be done at 'grass roots' level. Several requested local initiatives.

These principles and processes are now being applied to initiatives happening across Surrey and are directly involving local people in identifying and prioritising problems and generating solutions. The initial approach in Reigate and Banstead has engaged the business community along with other stakeholders and has generated many successful projects. A more 'bottom up' approach was adopted in North Guildford where the County Council Education Department initially worked with the Safer Surrey Partnership to gain other key services's support, in establishing three improvement projects covering employment, youth issues, parenting and literacy. This work has been sustained and developed over five years and now includes a significant input from the church in the community with ongoing support through a multi-agency group.

Stakeholding in Communities — Strong Relationships

When it comes to community-wide improvement relationship is everything. People are being brought together who are not used to working together. The stakeholders may not share the same history, language or agenda. Trust is key but this cannot be created quickly. Friction may not necessarily be undesirable. If managed, this tension can lead to very creative solutions. Conflicts will happen. Processes need to be developed for handling this conflict. The example of working with Native Americans by Harvey Stewart explores the need to build strong relationships. 'A Third World Nation within the United States' is presented in full at the end of this section.

Stakeholding in Communities — Sustainable Results

Achieving sustainable results in community-wide improvement is critical. Too many initiatives achieve initial results and are then concluded without ensuring that the results can be sustained and future improvements can be made. The Quality in the Community Project in Bristol has developed a plan for sustainability at the start, not towards the end.

There is no substitute for success. Real results and stakeholder benefits must be achieved and people must know and value these. There must be high levels of ownership founded on the community setting their own agenda. People must have a passion and determination to keep the ideals of the Project operating. QIC is proposing to use a 'contracting' process to achieve sustainability. It will be made very clear at the start of any work what is expected from each player. If the 'experts' are going to provide effective support they require certain things from the people getting involved. This is similar to the concepts being used by teachers and students in education. As already explored, people must be trained to ensure sustainability, but less formal mechanisms are required to continue to build capacity. QIC is proposing a coaching/mentoring process. People will shadow more experienced facilitators and there will be an informal network to develop new people. The aim is that the community will manage this process themselves. Communication and the sharing of information will be central to ensuring sustainability and the 'professionals' will try to ensure that any work links into the wider City picture. If the elements of this plan can be implemented there is a very good likelihood that the initial benefits will continue to flourish and the improvement process will be continuous rather than a 'one-off'.

Stakeholding in Communities – Sound Evaluation

Evaluation in communities is a real challenge. Funders tend to concentrate on outputs, whereas people in the communities care about outcomes. Project managers have to manage the potential tensions. Produce the results for the funders but establish community-driven indicators, which may be softer. How does one measure the impact of improved confidence for people who have been systematically excluded from participating in improving their communities? This will have profound knock-on effects on friends and family and represents the unknown or unknowable of community development. Softer indicators and examples will have to be used by community projects to demonstrate their real value until Ministers and Civil Servants learn about measurement.

A Third World nation within the United States

Harvey Stewart has written the following example. Harvey is Vice President of the Foundation for Community Vitality and the Co-ordinator for the North West Indian Ministry.

Travelling westward out of the northern plains of the Dakotas you enter the vast expanses of the mountain states. Lying against the Canadian border, the State of Montana stretches southward 400 miles, and fills the space between North Dakota and Idaho with 600 miles of great mountain ranges linked together by miles of rolling hills. It has been called a small town with long streets. It is rural, with the largest community claiming 90,000 residents. Set within this "Big Sky" country is the Nation of the Crow people - the Apsaalooke; the Crow Indian Reservation.

Once Crow country easily encompassed over 38 million acres. Now the boundaries contain less than one-twentieth that amount as the pressures from a dominant culture continue to erode the land base of the Crow people. Located in the south central part of the state, the reservation is approximately 70 miles by 80 miles in size. Non-Indian ranchers own almost 50 percent of the land within the Reservation. Economically it is a dependent nation.

Indian reservations within the United States are often compared to Third World countries. Native Americans are the poorest housed, least educated, and most oppressed people group in the country. Unemployment on the Crow Reservation fluctuates between 65 and 95 percent. Suicide, substance abuse, mortality and teenage pregnancy rates are all three to five times greater than the national average. Retail leakage of income off the reservation into the surrounding communities is more like a flood than a leak. A long list of statistics can only serve to further substantiate the above and lengthen a general list of problems.

The majority of the income that flows into the Crow Reservation is through dependent relationships. Key income-producing activities are agriculture, mining, education, health care, and government. Agriculture primarily benefits the Crow people through land that is leased to non-native ranchers. The mining is owned and operated by someone else though it is on Crow land with royalties and taxes going to the Crow people. Education is publicly supported, as is health care, and the tribal government is basically dependent upon U.S. government programmes for its operation. There are very few Crow ranchers, and the number of business persons is nominal. This represents an economic system that sustains dependency.

The political system also sustains dependency. It was imposed upon the people, has little cultural relevance, and a two-year term for elected offices has a consistently destabilising effect. The tribal government is the major employer on the Reservation, and this can create a highly politicised environment with abuses. Although the tribal government searches for ways to build the economy, they have not focused on building the private sector. Instead, their businesses are government owned. This results in continuing the cycle of dependence. It may make a difference that the tribal government as the administrator and business owner has replaced the U.S. government, but the result on the individual tribal member is probably the same.

In the midst of these grim realities you find a vibrant people who have retained their culture and language as much or more than any tribe in the country. Though the Crow country is beautiful and resource rich, clearly the greatest resource is the people. Their tribal values, which relate to an economic system of the past, serve well their current social needs. Tension exists, however, between those values and the values supporting the economy of the larger society in the U.S. Much still needs to be learned about how to be competitive economically while appreciating and even utilising tribal values.

It is also important to understand that the social support system that strengthens economic development is very weak on the reservation. The establishment of reservations marked the end of traditional economic systems. Some elements may exist, but as a whole they are gone. In the past, adult people were not given a horse and a bow and arrows for the first time and told to go west to hunt some buffalo. There was a very elaborate educational process that all children went through to prepare them to participate in the economy of the Tribe. When the time came to hunt, trade, or raid, each person was well prepared and had a strong support system within their community.

Economic development on reservations today often takes the approach of giving the adult the equipment without either the skills or any social support system to help insure success. If you go to Billings, MT, which sits next to the northwest corner of the reservation, you will see something very different. As in most economically healthy communities there are many businesses. Children are surrounded by a broad variety of businesses owned by people of their own culture. Family members either own, or work for private sector businesses. Children hear conversations about those businesses, and probably have opportunities to visit with business people as they grow up. The educational system has intentional links with the private sector economy through content and educational experiences. There exists a direct relationship between education, future employment, and personal success.

All of these connections existed within the traditional economy of the Crows, but only fragments of that economy remain and those missing pieces must be replaced with appropriate systems for today. Due to such high unemployment, few businesses, and value systems that sometime conflict with the mainstream economy; the connection between education, employment and personal success is weak on the Reservation. My personal opinion is that traditional values need to be interpreted for use today, and something must provide an effective support system for a private sector based economy. If you took the value system of a Crow warrior and placed it within the business world of today, you would have a very aggressive business person. That person would be highly skilled. The community would provide solid support. Success would insure a deep commitment to the prosperity of the Crow people, and care not to damage the social and environmental systems that insure sustained economic health.

In respect of the Crow culture, the first step in beginning a working group is getting permission from the elders. Not because they might exercise some authority and ruin one's efforts, it is simply the right thing to do. So after visiting individually with several elders, and receiving their blessing, I began to visit with potential leaders. The first two were Dr. Janine Pease Pretty On Top, and Jim Scott. Janine is the president of Little Big Horn College, the Tribal College in Crow Agency, MT. Jim is the Vice-President of First Interstate Banc Systems in Billings, MT.

These actions represent the first steps in getting stakeholders involved. By visiting with these two people first, a strategy was suggested: that economic development would include partnerships between individuals and institutions on and off of the Reservation.

The process of expanding the stakeholder group was not very specific, and the use of the term "stakeholder" was rare, but the results were the same. Janine suggested others on the Reservation to be involved in the planning process. They included college staff, community business persons, community leaders, tribal government staff, and a county commissioner. This group constituted a kind of "think tank", and was called the "Crow Community Co-operative", for lack of a better name.

Prior to visiting with the elders I had written a concept paper about a small business loan process that might be culturally appropriate on the Reservation. It emphasised education, small business loans with community-led approval, and small groups of loan recipients providing mutual support and benefits connected to loan repayment for interrelated support services provided by the loan recipients. This simply served as a starting point. It was a little better than beginning with a blank piece of paper, but we were able to use it as a concept paper to receive a planning grant from a foundation of just under 20,000 dollars for one year. We hold the record for the longest one-year planning grant ever given by that foundation. For over two years we worked to understand the most appropriate way to begin supporting economic development among the Crow people.

During that time we consistently discussed issues related to the culture of the Crows. Developing a culturally appropriate program was clearly a critical factor for success. We also began to collect data from the community. Two surveys were conducted to determine the interest in small business loans by the students of the college, and several members of six different communities. We studied the existing economy on the reservation, and related issues. Outside expertise was also utilised as we looked at other small loan programs in the United States and Canada that worked with Native people. The result was a plan with a dual emphasis: circle banking and tourism.

Circle banking is a peer lending process, best known by the work of Dr. Muhamed Yunus in Bangladesh, called the Garmeen Bank. The best example of its application on an Indian reservation is the Lakota Fund, in Kyle, South Dakota, on the Pine Ridge Indian Reservation. The circle banking process usually includes small groups of five to seven people who each receive individual loans, but are corporately responsible for the repayment of one another's loan debt to the program. The groups are self-selected and are often formed out of mutual interest in a particular type of business. People in the same group may be in similar businesses, but they can not pool their loans for a single business. The loans are small and are made from a revolving loan fund.

Each person is usually required to attend workshops to understand the program and increase their business skills. The group selects its own leadership and the first person that will receive a loan. Sometimes the group is required to raise a portion of the loan as their investment capital and possibly a repayment reserve fund. Only after the first person has made a required number of payments on time, three or more, is the next person given their loan. This process continues until all the group members receive their loan. The group members often collect the loan payments during regular meetings, and submit them for their group. If any payments are late the group is responsible to make them and keep each loan repayment schedule up to date, or no further loans are available to the group.

The Crow Reservation loan program operated on the principles described above with several variations. In the interest of brevity I won't describe it in detail, but it may be helpful to know that the first loan could not exceed 400 dollars. After successfully paying off the first loan the amount available increased incrementally up to 2,000 dollars. At that time the local bank would consider assuming the loan relationship with the business person.

Tourism holds real growth potential on the Crow Reservation. Next to Crow Agency is the Little Big Horn BattleField. This is the location of the battle between the joined forces of several of the bands of the Sioux and Cheyenne Tribes led by famous chiefs, and the Seventh Calvary led by General George Armstrong Custer. It represents one of those historic events that continues to capture the interest of hundreds of thousands of people each year. In short, General Custer considered himself a premier Indian fighter. He chased them long enough to make them mad, and made some poor decisions that got him and all of his men quickly killed. This creates a known market for several types of businesses that serve tourists. A key ingredient is the interest that people have in Native Americans.

The tourism program focused on three areas: 1) providing the tours at the Little Big Horn Battle Field, a federal park; 2) providing a market for artisans to sell their products; 3) providing cultural awareness opportunities for tour groups in co-operation with off-reservation organisations. Any opportunities that existed for synergy between the programs were examined and implemented.

Both the loan program and tourism program was housed within Little Big Horn College. A staff person was hired and funds acquired through a program grant from a foundation. Staff members and faculty members of the college worked with the programs. Forming an Advisory Committee of community members, other business and public service persons expanded the stakeholder group.

Circle banking groups were formed, equipped, and the loan process was initiated. Tour groups began to be served, a small open-air market was provided for the artisans, and a contract was acquired to provide the step-on tours at the battlefield.

Throughout this process the implementation steps of plan-do-study-act (PDSA) were utilised in a limited form. The plans could not always be applied incrementally to the programs, and data was not as detailed as is desired for study before broad implementation. Some limits for this process existed within the time frame required by the foundation funding the project. A longer time line would have provided better opportunity to acquaint people with detailed data gathering and analysis tools. Some of the reason for this is the value-laden characteristic of any process that is introduced from one culture into another. It is an important point to keep in mind when working cross-culturally.

Evaluation, lessons learned and their application to achieve continuous improvement was accomplished by all involved. Staff persons, customers, the Advisory Council and community members all had input with co-ordination provided by the "think tank" group. Some of this was specific and solicited, other input was random. Periodic reviews of progress, processes, barriers and results were structured and directed toward improvement. We continued to look at the overall system for each aspect of the project, and the related systems within the collaborating institutions. Data was used for analysis, but limited staff resources prevented us from consistently having all the data we desired. Again, the PDSA cycle was used when possible.

The tourism project is operating in the black. The step-on tours at the battlefield have been successful. They have served as an excellent skill building experience for the students that have served as guides. The number of outside tour groups that are served has increased, and customer satisfaction continues to improve.

The circle-banking program was initiated within three communities. After three years of operation it was decided to move the focus within the college, working closely with the students, and connecting their business interests with their course work. The planning process for this continues as I write this case study. We anticipate strong partnerships with businesses, and improved economic stability to ensure sustainability of this program.

Chapter 15

The Future

I want to conclude this book with a review of two disturbing examples of lack of stakeholding and then a positive look at the future. The examples may, at first glance, appear a little obscure but they highlight many of the needs to consider the whole system.

The first example is the fable of the bus conductor, which is developed from an idea presented by Will Hutton (67). This is a micro example with macro implications. The story starts with the deregulation and privatisation of bus services. In the new regime the bus companies are under ever increasing pressures from shareholders to maximise their immediate dividends. This has led many companies to focus on cost cutting. One way to reduce short-term costs was to 'downsize' bus crews from driver plus conductor to driver-only crews. There were many consequences of this action, some foreseen, others not. The immediate benefit for the bus companies was the reduction of their staffing costs by making the conductors redundant. So the bus companies get a short-term 'win' and the shareholders a greater return on their investment. However, let us consider the impact on the wider system. The taxpayers, unfortunately, get an immediate 'loss' because social security and retraining costs rise, but there are other more subtle implications. Driver-only buses take longer to pick up passengers. The consequential delays reduce traffic flow. Other road users lose. Conductors did not only take fares; they provided many other services, not least of which was security. As a consequence of not having conductors, vandalism and violence is more common. Passengers feel less safe and hence their service is reduced — another loss. Bus companies start to experience increased costs of repair and the police experience greater pressures on their already limited resources. Eventually the public demands more law enforcement and the community picks up the tab. Greater social security and law enforcement costs means that there is less public money to invest in public transport. Eventually the bus companies will lose, too. The reduction in service may well lead to fewer people using buses and exacerbate congestion. Eventually everyone loses, even the shareholders. Unless the win/win solution can be found everyone will lose in the end. No one is suggesting running inefficient services but organisations need to consider the implications of their actions on the wider system and the less definable parts of their service. (This situation is summarised as a Relation Diagram in Figure 32.)

Environmentalists are key stakeholders in any change process. Easter Island may be an environmental microcosm of what could be happening on a global scale (68). This Pacific Island remained isolated from the rest of world for many centuries, so much so that inhabitants thought that the rest of the world had been destroyed. The example of what may have happened is a sobering lesson to us all. Many readers will be aware of the statues that exist on the island. It is thought that these statues had important religious meaning. They were also status symbols for competing tribes. In order to build statues there was a lot of pressure on natural resources, particularly trees. Trees were cut down in their hundreds to erect the statues. As a consequence the pressure on the environment increased. This sparked off many vicious circles. The first was that as food shortages increased competition between tribes increased. It is believed that this led to violent conflicts and as a result more of the environment and crops were destroyed. As pressure for food increased more land was cleared for agriculture leading to more destruction of the palm trees. It is speculated that other food sources were pillaged. The bird and fish population started to decline rapidly. With the arrival of the Europeans, rats were introduced as a food source. Unfortunately the rats destroyed more trees, exacerbating the very problem they were supposed to alleviate. This led to more conflict and the spiral of decline continued eventually resulting in the collapse of the inhabitants' religious system. At some point either through conflict or disillusionment the statues were toppled and have only recently been reinstated. Through lack of systems thinking and co-operation the whole social and environmental system collapsed. This is summarised in Figure 33, a Relation Diagram of the decline of Easter Island.

It is possible to view almost the whole of Easter Island from the highest vantage point. The most sobering thought is that someone must have cut down the last tree. They probably knew that it was the last one. They may have had an idea of the implications but they still went ahead and did it! Is there a lesson from Easter Island? Can mankind co-operate and learn that for every action there are many reactions? Let's hope so. Stakeholding is not some ideal dream. It might just be a pre-requisite for survival.

On a more positive note there is optimism for the future. A tidal wave of change is sweeping the world. Communism has collapsed but capitalism is not the victor, its competitor just happened to decline first. Rampant capitalism is unsustainable. Even the most ruthless of corporations are waking up to the need to consider the whole system and to engage all stakeholders in a meaningful way. Inclusive models are being developed all over the world. Let us hope that the prevalent system allows them to flourish and that we don't use the flawed paradigms to measure the new ones.

One knows when one is on a major 'paradigm shift' when the old solutions cannot solve the new problems. People start to innovate and this can be a painful process. As we enter the new millennium the world is on the verge of a major shift. Our prevalent world views have to adapt otherwise we, like the Easter Islanders, will be tearing down our monuments in disillusionment too. We need to adopt stakeholding not just as a concept but as a practical way of working. Listen to the message that history sends us and then we can demonstrate what an adaptive species we are.

All over the world people, from all walks of life, are 'planting trees'. These pioneers, influenced by intellectuals like Deming, Hutton, Etzioni and Covey, are applying new methods, based on interdependence and stakeholding, in business, education, government and communities. They are turning upside down some of our traditional ideas and proving that there are better, more people-centred, ways of doing things. As we enter a new period of history there is an emerging optimism that we will adapt to the challenges that we, as a global community, face.

Have you ever watched the ocean when the tide changes direction? It is a messy process. A lot of rubbish is brought to the surface, but at this point you can be sure that the direction is changing! Are you, as leaders, prepared to be a part of the tidal change or are you just going to watch?

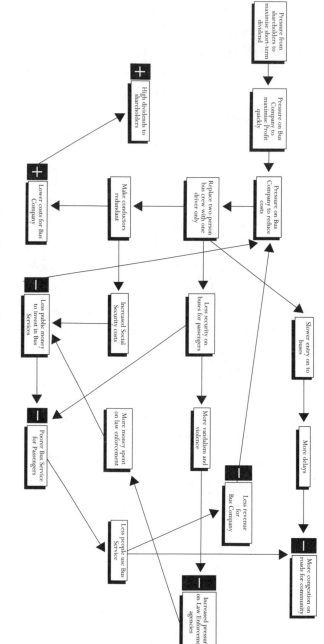

Figure 32. Relation Diagram of the Parable of the Bus Conductor

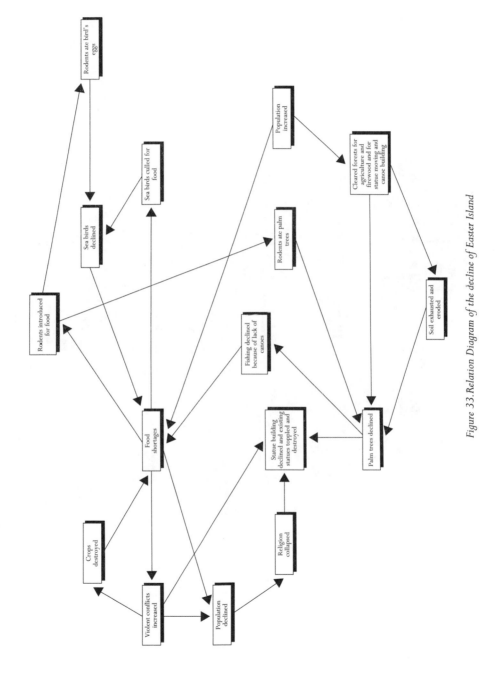

Figure 33. Relation Diagram of the decline of Easter Island

References

(1)   Hutton, W., *The State We're In*, Jonathon Cape, 1995.

(2)   Deming, W. E., *The New Economics for Industry, Government and Education*, MIT, CAES, 1993.

(3)   Barker, J., *Future Edge*, Morrow, 1992.

(4)   Kuhn, T. S., *The Structure of Scientific Revolutions*, University of Chicago Press, 1970.

(5)   Walsh, B. J. & Middleton, J. R., *The Transforming Vision*, Inter-Varsity Press, 1984, page 31.

(6)   Deming, W. E., *The New Economics for Industry*, Government and Education, MIT, CAES, 1993, page 125.

(7)   RSA Inquiry, *Tomorrow's Company: The Role of Business in a Changing World*, RSA, 1994, page 2.

(8)   Deming, W. E., *Out of the Crisis*, Cambridge University Press, 1986, page 121.

(9)   Etzioni, A., *The Spirit of Community - the Reinvention of American Society*, Simon & Schuster, 1993.

(10)   Deming, W. E., *The New Economics for Industry, Government and Education*, MIT, CAES, 1993, page 51.

(11)   RSA Inquiry, *Tomorrow's Company: The Role of Business in a Changing World, RSA*, 1994, page 2.

(12)   Deming, W. E., *The New Economics for Industry, Government and Education*, MIT, CAES, 1993, page 98.

(13)   Handy, C. B., *The Age of Unreason*, Harvard Business School Press, 1990, page 46.

(14)   Covey, S. R., *Principle Centred Leadership*, Summit, 1991, page 251.

(15) Attributed to the late Larrae Rocheleau, former Superintendent, Mt Edgecumbe High School.

(16) Carlisle, J. A. & Parker, R. C., *Beyond Negotiation – Redeeming Customer-Supplier Relationships*, John Wiley & Sons, 1989, page 154.

(17) Deming, W. E., *Out of the Crisis*, Cambridge University Press, 1986, page 59.

(18) Deming, W. E., *Out of the Crisis*, Cambridge University Press, 1986, page 24.

(19) Wheeler, D. J., *Advanced Topics in Statistical Process Control*, SPC Press, 1995, page 199.

(20) Senge, P. M., *The Fifth Discipline*, Doubleday, 1990, page 63.

(21) Equal *Opportunities Quality Framework*, The Equality Foundation, WESTEC, 1995.

(22) RSA Inquiry, Tomorrow's Company: *The Role of Business in a Changing World*, RSA, 1994.

(23) RSA Inquiry, Tomorrow's Company: *The Role of Business in a Changing World*, RSA, 1994.

(24) Pirsig, R. M., *Zen and the Art of Motorcycle Maintenance*, Vantage, 1974.

(25) Senge, P. M., *The Fifth Discipline*, Doubleday, 1990, page 68.

(26) Department of the Environment, *Involving Communities in Urban and Rural Regeneration*, 1996.

(27) Department of the Environment, *Involving Communities in Urban and Rural Regeneration*, 1996.

(28) Marsh, J., 'Economics to Fight Decline', *Managing Service Quality*, MCB University Press, Nov., 1993, pages 15-20.

(29) Attributed to Brian Walsh, Institute for Christian Studies, Toronto, Canada.

(30) Deming, W. E., *Out of the Crisis*, Cambridge University Press, 1986, page 121.

(31) Marsh, J., *The Quality Toolkit*, Rushmere Wynne, 1996.

(32) Deming, W. E., *Out of the Crisis*, Cambridge University Press, 1986, page 121.

(33) Wheeler, D. J., *Advanced Topics in Statistical Process Control*, SPC Press, 1995, page 199.

(34)   Deming, W. E., *The New Economics for Industry, Government and Education*, MIT, CAES, 1993, page 219.

(35)   Wheeler, D. J., *Short Run SPC*, SPC Press, 1991, page 57.

(36)   Deming, W. E., *Out of the Crisis*, Cambridge University Press, 1986, page 318.

(37)   Deming, W. E., *Out of the Crisis*, Cambridge University Press, 1986, page 318.

(38)   Wheeler, D. J., *Understanding Variation – the key to managing chaos*, SPC Press, 1993, page 35.

(39)   Carlisle, J. A. & Parker, R. C., *Beyond Negotiation - Redeeming Customer-Supplier Relationships*, John Wiley & Sons, 1989, page 17.

(40)   Covey, S. R., *The Seven Habits of Highly Effective People*, Simon and Schuster, 1989.

(41)   Covey, S. R., *The Seven Habits of Highly Effective*, People, Simon and Schuster, 1989.

(42)   Berne, E., *Transactional Analysis in Psychotherapy*, Souvenir Press, 1975.

(43)   Hakes, C., *The Self Assessment Handbook*, Chapman & Hall, 1994.

(44)   British Quality Foundation, *Guides to Self-Assessment*, Updated annually.

(45)   Deming, W. E., *Out of the Crisis*, Cambridge University Press, 1986.

(46)   Covey, S. R., *The Seven Habits of Highly Effective People*, Simon and Schuster, 1989.

(47)   Deming, W. E., *The New Economics for Industry, Government and Education*, MIT, CAES, 1993, page 94.

(48)   Adair, J., *Not Bosses but Leaders*, Talbot Adair, 1987, page 51.

(49)   Deming, W. E., *Out of the Crisis*, Cambridge University Press, 1986, page 88.

(50)   Hutton, W., *The State We're In*, Jonathon Cape, 1995, page 230.

(51)   Rust, T. R., Zahorik, A. J. & Keiningham T. L., *Return on Quality*, Probus, 1994, page 33.

(52)   Deming, W. E., *Out of the Crisis*, Cambridge University Press, 1986, page 121.

(53)   Owen, H., *Open Space Technology – A User's Guide*, Abbott, 1992.

(54)   Weisbord, M. R. & Janoff, S., *Future Search*, Berett-Koehler, 1995.

(55)   Marsh, J., *The Quality Toolkit*, Rushmere Wynne, 1996.

(56)   Wheeler, D. J., *Understanding Variation – the key to managing chaos*, SPC Press, 1993, page 35.

(57)   Buzan, T., *Using Your Head*, BBC Books, 1974.

(58)   De Bono, E., *Serious Creativity*, Harper Collins, 1992.

(59)   Thomson, C., *What a Great Idea*, Harper Perennial, 1992.

(60)   Hewson, J. & Turner, C., *Transactional Analysis in Management*, The Staff College, 1992.

(61)   Carlisle, J. A. & Parker, R. C., *Beyond Negotiation – Redeeming Customer-Supplier Relationships*, John Wiley & Sons, 1989, page 88.

(62)   Survey conducted by Vanguard Consulting, 1992.

(63)   Hakes, C., *The Self Assessment Handbook*, Chapman & Hall, 1994.

(64)   Block, P., *Stewardship*, Berett-Koehler, 1993.

(65)   Etzioni, A., *The Spirit of Community – the Reinvention of American Society*, Simon & Schuster, 1993.

(66)   Handy, C. B., *The Age of Unreason*, Harvard Business School Press, 1990, page 211.

(67)   Hutton, W., *The State to Come*, Vintage, 1997, page 19.

(68)   Bahn, P. & Flenley, J., *Easter Island, Earth Island*, Thames and Hudson, 1992.

Feedback

This book contains some controversial ideas. The examples are drawn from the author's experience. In the spirit of continual improvement and learning, I would like to encourage people to respond and give feedback. Please let me know your suggestions for improvement and of other examples of best practice. I can be contacted as follows.

John Marsh
Total Quality Partnerships
84 Brackendene
Bradley Stoke
Bristol
BS12 9DH
United Kingdom

Telephone: +44 (0)1454 619496
Fax: +44 (0)1454 619487
Email: john@marshj.demon.co.uk
WWW: tqp.com

Index